Shakespeare
For All

David Irvin

Pen Press

First published in Great Britain by Pen Press

All paper used in the printing of this book has been made from wood grown in managed, sustainable forests.

ISBN13: 978-1-78003-687-8
Printed and bound in the UK
Pen Press is an imprint of
Indepenpress Publishing Limited
25 Eastern Place
Brighton
BN2 1GJ

A catalogue record of this book is available from the British Library

Cover design by Jacqueline Abromeit

For Nykki and Thomas

CONTENTS

All dates are slightly speculative, but are indicative of when Shakespeare is most likely to have finished writing the play.

INTRODUCTION

This is a book, in the form of a series of essays, about the plays Shakespeare wrote from 1599 onwards – almost exactly halfway through, in both years and output, his writing life. Its origins were a music class I attended on how different composers – Berlioz, Verdi and Tchaikovsky for example – explored Shakespearean characters or themes in their music. The tutor was Michael Chandler and the bulk of the group consisted of retired middle-class professionals; they were intelligent and literate and knew far more about music than I did, but though interested, possessed only a passing knowledge of Shakespeare's plays. So these essays, which are basically a personal response to the plays, are for intelligent people who want to know more about the plays and, I hope, will subsequently be encouraged to see professional productions of the plays. This target audience also includes sixth formers and first year university students: people just beginning to get their teeth into Shakespeare.

I don't think that any informed, intelligent person would dispute the claim that Shakespeare was the greatest playwright who ever lived. I think Coleridge got it absolutely right[1] when he wrote of "our myriad-minded Shakespeare" who was in possession of "the largest and most comprehensive soul". I will expand on this soon, but I think I need to explain why I am writing about only the second half of Shakespeare's playwriting; about the sequence of the essays and a couple of omissions.

In the first place, eighteen is a more manageable number of plays to discuss than thirty-six, and I had no intention of being comprehensive. The majority of plays written in the first half of Shakespeare's career are history plays and are performed less often, although they all yield something valuable to the audience. And, as James Shapiro

1   In *Biographia Literaria*.

convincingly explains in his excellent book *1599*, the year 1599 marked the opening of the Globe Theatre and the real success, and the established greatness, of Shakespeare. It is true that *Henry V* was probably written in 1599 and yet I have ignored it because it is the last play in the tetralogy of *Richard II, Henry IV Parts 1 and 2* and *Henry V*, and to have included it would have meant a discussion of the other three plays too. It is also true that by imposing 1599 as a cut-off point I have said nothing about plays such as *The Taming of the Shrew, Romeo and Juliet, A Midsummer Night's Dream* and *The Merchant of Venice*. I would simply say that they are among the most accessible of Shakespeare's plays, and certainly *Romeo and Juliet* and *A Midsummer Night's Dream* are pretty straightforward, with no complex issues, and are excellent starters for someone coming to Shakespeare for the first time.

I have also omitted *Henry VIII*. It was written after *The Tempest* and there is little doubt that at least half of it was written by John Fletcher. And not only is it a history play and therefore reminiscent of the first half of Shakespeare's playwriting, I also think it completely fitting that *The Tempest* should be registered as his last play! You will also find no discussion of *The Merry Wives of Windsor*. There are a number of reasons for this: firstly I don't think it is a very good play; secondly – although the theory that it was written at the express command of Queen Elizabeth, as she wanted to see Falstaff again and in love, was voiced for the first time in 1702 and therefore seems unlikely – there is an obvious link with the pre 1599 Prince Hal and Falstaff-centred plays; and thirdly, and most persuasively, the current thinking is that it was written before 1600, most likely in 1597. Otherwise all the plays you will find conventionally listed as being written from 1599 onwards are discussed – all eighteen of them.

The sequence, though, is not chronological. The main reason for this is that I was finding links between plays as I was writing; one play seemed to lead on to the next in my mind. The sequence emerged: just over halfway through I knew what my last three plays would be, but otherwise there was an ongoing excitement in the uncertainty about which would be the next play. The obvious question, though, is why start with *Coriolanus*? In 2012 I published another book[2] about

2   *Novels for Ed,* Grosvenor House Press 2012.

the novel, in which my thesis was that politicians should read novels rather than economic tomes: that way they would keep in touch with people and their needs and increase their understanding, sympathy, tolerance and acceptance of what it is to be human, through reading about the vast range of people that neither they nor any of us ever come into contact with in our everyday, rather limited life. This book on Shakespeare's plays began with the same premise and *Coriolanus* (together with *Julius Caesar*) is the most overtly political of those plays – and therefore a very good place to start. As happened with my book on the novel, the focus soon shifted from the learning that politicians could take from the novel to the learning that all mankind can take. So in this series of essays the explicit political relevance in the plays is naturally taken over by the relevance to everyman. If the book is read straight through from beginning to end I think that is apparent, but of course, the book is designed to be dipped into too, as each essay is self-contained.

I have a very mixed collection of Shakespeare's plays, by which I mean that every time I saw a Shakespeare play I bought a text of the play and some days I had more money than others. So when I have quoted from the text in these essays it is from the particular edition I have at hand – mainly it will be the Arden Shakespeare or the Signet edition but there are a few other editions too. Occasionally I have mentioned where the Quarto (individual) text and the Folio (collected) texts differ, but otherwise I have stayed with the more usual reading. I had absolutely no intention of writing a scholarly work: I hope what I have written is intelligent and informed, but fundamentally I am an enthusiast and a Shakespeare lover and not an academic. My aim is that my enthusiasm is communicated and that people are thereby encouraged to pursue Shakespeare for themselves.

What is so wonderful about Shakespeare's plays is his human understanding, which he presents and explores in frequently memorable verse and an enthralling dramatic context; so he entertains and makes us wiser at the same time. And he does this consistently throughout the body of his work. His contemporary Ben Jonson writes of his being the "soule of the age" but then adds: "He was not of an age but for all time."[3] Let me just mention a few

3   *Essays of Dramatic Poesy.*

of the everlasting themes that Shakespeare explores.

There is the political point made by Sicinius in *Coriolanus*: "What is the city but the people?" What are the principles behind governance and making laws? "Nothing emboldens sin so much as mercy," suggests the First Senator in *Timon of Athens*.

Shakespeare possesses so much basic wisdom apropos human behaviour. From Dogberry's (in *Much Ado About Nothing*) "they that touch pitch shall be defiled" through Iago's comment to Othello: "O beware jealousy; / It is the green-eyed monster, which doth mock / The meat it feeds on" to Prospero in *The Tempest* and his final realisation that "the rarer action is in virtue than in vengeance" the plays are full of insights about human behaviour and qualities.

Amongst the multiplicity of mankind we find in these plays, there is a place for cynics too. We hear Autolycus in *The Winter's Tale* expressing the belief that "what a fool Honesty is! and Trust, his sworn brother, a very simple gentleman". And is it honesty for the Shepherd in the same play to voice the opinion "Would there be no age between ten and three-and-twenty, or that youth would sleep out the rest; for there is nothing in the between but getting wenches with child, wronging the ancientry, stealing, fighting"? Is that cynicism or realism? We could ask the same question of Rosalind's statement in *As You Like It*: "Men have died from time to time and worms have eaten them, but not for love."

Shakespeare points out the glib hypocrisy that self-righteous establishment figures tend to have when he gives Angelo in *Measure for Measure* the words: "'Tis one thing to be tempted, Escalus, / Another thing to fall."

The pain experienced in relationships is seen in Lear's "How sharper than a serpent's tooth it is / To have a thankless child." As ever Shakespeare speaks for all men.

Yet he understands love. As Cressida in *Troilus and Cressida* laments, "to be wise in love / Exceeds man's might: that dwells with the gods above". And the Clown in *Twelfth Night* sings: "Then, come kiss me, sweet and twenty: / Youth's a stuff will not endure."

But love – in this case father and daughter love – can produce ecstasy; an almost out-of-body experience, as we hear Pericles, amazed: "The music of the spheres… I hear the music of the spheres."

The acknowledgment of the importance of time in all its dimensions is shown when Macbeth says: "The night is long that never finds the day." That maybe gives some hope, but then there is also the beautiful resignation in the song from *Cymbeline*: "Golden lads and girls all must / As chimney-sweepers, come to dust."

We are encouraged too to take responsibility for our own lives when Shakespeare gives to Cassius in *Julius Caesar* the words: "The fault, dear Brutus, is not in our stars, / But in ourselves that we are underlings."

Above all, I think, is the acceptance of human frailty and fallibility. Agrippa in *Antony and Cleopatra* points out that "You gods will give us some faults to make us men" and Hamlet explodes: "Use every man after his desert and who shall scape whipping."

This is the all-seeing, all-forgiving Shakespeare. This is what caused Laurence Olivier to claim that Shakespeare was "the nearest thing in incarnation to the eye of God". I have just listed some of the themes, with relevant quotations from all the plays I am discussing in this book, but they are mere bullet points: they are all expanded in the different essays. I hope they will lead the reader to the plays and to experience the intelligence and breadth of understanding and vision of Shakespeare. I have not gone down the route of linking the plays with the personal life: I think that is an unprofitable route to take with any artist, and besides we in reality know so little of Shakespeare's life. What we do know is that at eighteen he married a pregnant woman seven years older than he was and later lost his only son Hamnet at the age of eleven. That is all we need to know, for as Dryden[4] wrote: "He was not naturally learned, he needed not the spectacle of books to read nature. He looked inwards and found her there."

---

4   *Of Dramatic Poesy, 1668.*

CORIOLANUS

Coriolanus is about hubris – that overweening sense of self-pride and contempt for those who are perceived as lesser mortals, which, in a just world, brings about its own downfall. In the ancient Greek theatre this putting yourself (at the very least) on the same level as the gods would inevitably bring about nemesis, retribution from the gods for your arrogance and presumption in challenging the natural hierarchy of life. Although Coriolanus is a Roman general his biography is fully detailed in the Greek Plutarch's *Parallel Lives*, translated by Sir Thomas North and published in 1579 – the basic source of all Shakespeare's Roman plays.

So why is this play relevant to the Milibands and the Camerons, or indeed all politicians or anyone who by chance (which they tend to interpret as "my own hard work, skills and exceptional qualities") attains a position of power? For me there are two main reasons, and the first is as an example of how success breeds vanity and how power corrupts. I know that that is stating the bleeding obvious: examples abound throughout history, from ancient times to Mugabe, Gaddafi, Saddam Hussein, Assad etc. today. What I would hope is that an imagined world will have more of an impact on the audience member than any bare facts of history that politicians have forgotten or indeed never knew.[5] Plus, whatever the faults of Coriolanus, he can be praised for refusing to prostitute himself for the sake of consolidating his pride and power. What we all need to learn is how

---

5   I am reminded of Tony Blair's total ignorance about Mosaddeq, the Iranian Prime Minister who nationalised the Anglo-Iranian Oil Company in 1951 and was usurped by the Shah in an uprising encouraged by the United Kingdom in 1953. Talking to Jon Snow about the problems current with Iran he revealed a disturbing lack of knowledge about past history.

seductive is power and how it distorts our understanding of the real world.

And that is the second point of learning from *Coriolanus*. There are always citizens, ordinary people who, together with the rulers, form the body politic. Coriolanus has nothing but contempt for their cowardice, fickleness and turpitude. By alienating the mass of people and not wishing them to have a share of government Coriolanus is contributing to an unhealthy, unhappy state. That people need to be heard and need to be seen to have some kind of input into political debates is a moral of *Coriolanus*. I think all who hold the levers of power cannot hear this too often. (I am writing this – February 12th 2012 – when Syrian dissidents are being bombed into silence in Homs and other towns, when the Greek parliament appears to be about to vote for the draconic measures imposed on it by the Eurozone and the IMF despite the protests of the people, and when the British coalition government appears hell-bent on pushing through 'reforms' of the National Health Service, against the wishes of all informed opinion and effectively privatising it. By the time this essay is published these examples will be dated, but I have no doubt that similar ones will be found.)

There is no subplot in *Coriolanus*. Caius Marcus, encouraged by his mother Volumnia, has fought valiantly and successfully for Rome in eighteen campaigns since he was sixteen. In the play he defeats the Volscians, and their leader Aufidius, gloriously, capturing the town of Corioli and thereby earning the name Coriolanus. On his return he is to be made consul, but this involves what he sees as pandering to the townspeople: he sees them as rabble, shows his contempt for them and is banished. He then joins up with his long-time foe Aufidius, vowing revenge on Rome and a wish to burn it to the ground. The moving and impassioned pleading of Volumnia eventually persuades him to spare Rome. He signs a peace treaty, is accused of betrayal by the Volscians and killed by Aufidius' men.

Coriolanus is full of political resonances. The play opens with a famine in Rome, for which, despite Menenius laying responsibility on the gods, the citizens of Rome blame the patricians (the Roman nobility) for their selfishness in failing to distribute fairly the food (and wealth?)[6]. The citizens are also unhappy about the removal of restraints on usury (moneylending). Laws too are being passed giving more freedom to the rich and enchaining even further the poor. The patrician Menenius is trying to reason with and placate the mob, but Coriolanus – or Caius Marcius as he then was – will have none of it. After insulting the bravery and the judgment of the crowd he further scorns them with: "They'll sit by th' fire and presume to know / What's done i' th' Capitol."

Personally he wishes the nobility to put aside their compassion and permit him to use his sword against the dissenting mob. Later in the play, after his successful campaign against the Volscians, he reluctantly agrees to adhere to the custom of showing his wounds to the people – wounds that he received on behalf of Rome – thereby ensuring the crowd's endorsement of him as consul. The audience hears again his scorn for the people as he comments to Menenius on their personal hygiene and his having "to beg of Hob and Dick".

So on the one hand we have an overbearingly proud leader, contemptuous of the hoi polloi, and on the other a fickle, easily discredited mob. I use the word fickle because in the scene I have outlined, at the end of the last paragraph Coriolanus initially obtains the voices of the citizens supporting him as consul. But in just about the twinkling of an eye, they are convinced by the peoples' tribunes, Sicinius and Brutus, that he had mocked them and they very nearly "passed him unelected". Brutus points out that when he had no power: "He was your enemy, ever spake against / Your liberties."

Coriolanus is thus immediately deselected. The rumbling discontent of the populace means that the prospect of civil war appears to hang over Rome – which prospect is not enough in itself for Coriolanus to venture once more before the people until he is persuaded to do so by the impassioned pleadings of his mother. But he cannot sustain the humble role required of him and, confronted with Sicinius calling him "a traitor to the people", he explodes: "You common cry of curs, whose breath I hate / As reek o' the rotten fens, whose loves I prize / As the dead carcasses of unburied men / That do corrupt my air, I banish you."

---

6   The inequalities of wealth and the unfairness of its distribution are seen throughout the world today from the UK to the USA to India.

There is no doubting the character blemishes of Coriolanus, but what about the mob? Easily swayed by the voices of their tribunes, easily aroused to rebellion, perhaps they are worthy of the contempt and scorn heaped upon them by Coriolanus. And maybe Brutus and Sicinius are the equivalent of rabble-rousing trade union leaders with no understanding and no feelings of responsibility vis-à-vis their role in the state? Some critics have seen Shakespeare's critical presentation of the Roman populace as an indication of his own sympathies lying with the patricians, but as D. A. Traversi[7] points out: "We are shown a populace incapable of discerning its own good, vicious and vulgar, and needing the leadership of a class superior to itself. On the other hand, we are also shown a patrician class who have forfeited their right to superiority by showing a complete selfishness and lack of responsibility." (Remember we are told at the outset of *Coriolanus* that there is a famine in Rome, and that the people are deprived of bread which is being stored by the patricians for themselves.) But the throng are clearly easily led – it should therefore not have been a problem for the patricians to get them on side. As A. C. Bradley points out in his essay on *Coriolanus*: "they not only follow their tribunes like sheep; they receive abuse and direction submissively from anyone who shows goodwill. They are fundamentally good-natured, like the Englishmen they are, and have a humorous consciousness of their own weaknesses. They are beyond doubt mutable, and in that sense untrustworthy; but they are not by nature ungrateful, or slow to admire their bitterest enemy."

I think the fundamental point is that on both sides of the political divide there are faults, but in *Coriolanus* if you forget about Coriolanus, Brutus and Sicinius, reconciliation within the body politic would seem to be obtainable. Without those three, though, we would not have a play! So let us turn to the play for the last words on this political subject: they are spoken by Menenius who represents the voice of reason. Very early in the play he uses the image of the body and the belly – how the belly (the patricians) "is the storehouse and the shop of the whole body", but then the belly distributes the food through the rivers of blood to enable all the other parts of the body to function. The belly/patricians provide the logistics for the body/state to function. Menenius' claim is: "you shall find / No public

7   *An Approach to Shakespeare*, 1969.

benefit which you receive / But it proceeds or comes from them [the senators of Rome] to you".

Obviously there is something patronizing in Menenius' analogy, but it could well be the starting point for a real dialogue involving all levels of society. Indeed, this is one of the main reasons for seeing *Coriolanus*: it can open up a debate about the nature of democracy and the way we treat each other. For me the issue is one of respect. At some level – maybe an unconscious one – those who wield power can gain a good deal from seeing the flawed workings of government in *Coriolanus*.

That, however, is not the only learning to be had – there is the character of Coriolanus himself. How he differs – and it is a significant difference – from those we would classify as Shakespeare's tragic heroes (Hamlet, Othello, Lear, Macbeth) is that there is no introspection, no apparent self-awareness. We simply see him in public: never do we see him nursing any doubts. His valour and military expertise are not in question, but then neither is his hubris nor his pig-headed one-dimensional view of life. Shyness and vanity are good bedfellows and it is true that rather than hear the Senate sing his praises he briefly absences himself, but his pride and despising of the plebeians are not in doubt: wearing the gown of humility is anathema to him. (It is interesting that Shakespeare has made Coriolanus more extreme than he was presented in Plutarch's *Parallel Lives*: in Plutarch he does show his wounds to the people and there is no mention of the threat he makes in this play to burn down Rome. In all his plays Shakespeare uses his sources freely and imaginatively, e.g. in *Coriolanus* he lifts Menenius' speech about the belly and the functions of the body almost straight from Plutarch, but whereas Plutarch does not mention Menenius again Shakespeare develops his character – though not to the extent that Ralph Fiennes does in his recent film *Coriolanus*, in which we witness Menenius committing suicide after his failed attempt to persuade Coriolanus not to avenge himself on Rome.)

So we have a one-dimensional, self-satisfied, highly successful military leader who cannot see a gram of truth in Sicinius' words: "What is the city but the people?" It is a wilful failure to understand; a refusal to countenance anything like a compromise. Perhaps a lack of intelligence? In so far as recent research has shown that intelligence is more likely to be an attribute of left-wing thinkers and that those on the right are likely to be less intelligent, we can see how Coriolanus fits in with this theory: he believes he is born to exercise power, exhibits no self-doubt and is prepared to bring himself and his city down in defence of his authoritarian beliefs. Assuredly there is so much in *Coriolanus* for politicians et al. to ponder on: what effect does success have on the ego, for example, and how can the power of a leader be curbed rather than aggrandized?

Before we look at some of the questions raised in *Coriolanus* about war and the macho world that is presented, there is what we could call the Freudian question to consider. The only person that Coriolanus will listen to and be moved by is his mother – not his wife, nor the eminently reasonable Menenius, but his mother and she alone. She it is who encouraged his quest for military glory; from an early age it would have been laid upon him thickly: "I had rather had eleven die nobly for their country than one voluptuously surfeit out of action." It has proved impossible for Coriolanus to free himself from the indoctrination he has received from his mother; her love up to now would appear to have been conditional on his military success, and as Coriolanus has had military success in abundance the bond between them has been constantly cemented by Coriolanus' military glory. Even in the speech which eventually persuades Coriolanus to sign a peace treaty, Volumnia - incidentally portrayed wonderfully by Vanessa Redgrave in the film previously referred to – talks of his honour "to imitate the graces of the gods". It is a dangerous closeness that Coriolanus and Volumnia have: "There's no man in the world / More bound t's mother" – Volumnia's words. Coriolanus is a man who has not been permitted to think freely for himself. Such men are dangerous.

Coriolanus raises issues too about the nature and uses of war. Volumnia, the most vociferous advocate of the honour to be attained through military success, is nonetheless able to see that honour and peacemaking are also compatible. Then we have the comments from Aufidius' serving men to the effect that peace is unbearably dull and that it is "a getter of more bastard children than war's a destroyer of men". And at the heart of *Coriolanus* is the belief that a successful general is ipso facto worthy of the highest honours – a belief which Coriolanus accepts unquestioningly. In this context it is interesting that the British public did not, after the Second World War and despite expectations, elect Churchill, the successful war leader, to the post of Prime Minister, though subsequently he vies with Shakespeare in any poll as being the greatest Briton – the one encompasses, with acceptance and tolerance, all that is good and complex in human nature; the other was demonstratively racist, anti-trade union (the populace in *Coriolanus*) – and yet a great leader in times of war.

It could be argued too that the patricians are pleased to have to fight a war against the Volsci – war unites the city and removes the likelihood of the prospective food riots. One can see a parallel in 20th century Britain when Margaret Thatcher's government chose to go to war against Argentina over the Falkland Islands/Malvinas in 1982. Before that she had the lowest popularity ratings of any Prime Minister ever, but after what she saw as a triumphant campaign such was her popularity that she was able to defeat the miners in 1984 and then impose on British society her blueprint, which many would argue was a blueprint for selfishness and unmitigated greed.

You don't have to agree with that last statement but I think you have to acknowledge that this play provides so much food for political thought – thought which is so much easier because we are distanced by time and a script from the events. It makes it easier for principles to be established. *Coriolanus* in addition asks the question: "What price patriotism?" The patricians see Coriolanus as a great patriot, a great fighter for his city, yet the first words spoken about him by the citizens of Rome are that he is "chief enemy to the people". Matters are never simple. And then this great patriot, when not given the recognition he is sure he deserves, turns his back on his city and is prepared to burn it to the ground. So much for patriotism. Does it as a concept have any value other than to encourage the enjoyment of fighting? Patricians and the crowd can be equally fickle.

There is one other issue that *Coriolanus* brings up that I think is important for all of us to consider. As in so many of Shakespeare's plays – and as was inevitable with boys playing the female roles in Elizabethan theatre – there are questions of blurred sexuality. There is no cross-dressing in this play, but we need to look at the relationship between Coriolanus and Aufidius. I am thinking especially of the words with which Aufidius greets Coriolanus when he defects to the Volsci: "…that I see thee here, / Thou noble thing, more dances my rapt heart / Than when I first my wedded mistress saw / Bestride my threshold". This after he has twined his arms around Coriolanus' body. Later, the Third Servingman talks of Coriolanus being welcomed "as if he were son and heir to Mars" and then how Aufidius seems to worship him like a mistress, touches his hand and rolls his eyes at him as though he were something divine. If we wish to pursue the possible homoeroticism of *Coriolanus* we could adduce the greeting Coriolanus gives to his fellow general Cominius in the first Act after the defeat of the Volsci, when he says he is as happy as he was when bedtime approached on his wedding night.

Actually, I think the quest for homoerotic meaning in *Coriolanus* takes us down a cul-de-sac. What is significant is that the examples to which I have referred are all delighted greetings between generals; military men, and what is being celebrated is their shared values in the male, macho, military world. It is a world in which it is a given that men are inherently superior to women. It's the all-boys-together approach, found mainly in any army in the world but also in rugby and football clubs, which is at the heart of using and raping women. Being a soldier gives you supreme power and the freedom to express your power. Love for women cannot equate to the bond of camaraderie that exists between those doing battle together and women had better not get in your way – though a sentimental attachment is allowed to your own mother, wife and daughters. Military values? They need to be questioned.

Which is what Shakespeare is doing in *Coriolanus*. It is all very well for George Bernard Shaw[8] to sneer at *Coriolanus* as being Shakespeare's finest comedy but in reality we have the depiction of a military egomaniac taken to extremes, and the consequences thereof. Unless you first and foremost possess humility then you have nothing else of value to contribute to society…

Hubris is Coriolanus' fatal flaw – he does not question the aptness

---

8   Shaw was always intent on claiming his greatness was more than was Shakespeare's. He exulted in putting Shakespeare down.

of Menenius' having "godded me". Temperament is fate, and Shakespeare follows this central tenet of Plutarch's. Coriolanus is not depraved in the way that, for example, Seneca's Atreus[9] is depraved, but around the story of Coriolanus Shakespeare has woven a desperate and warring society which raises political issues for all societies. Seeing such a play can be an invaluable experience.

Neither the rashness of ambition, nor the fickle favour of the populace can ever sway him – this is apropos the desirable qualities for a king and no one has supporters rich enough that he can guarantee himself tomorrow.

---

9   Atreus killed his brother Thyestes' children and served them to an unaware Thyestes at a banquet.

Memorable Quotations From *Coriolanus*

I speak this in hunger for bread, not in thirst for revenge.
(First Citizen)

What's the matter, you dissentious rogues
That, rubbing the poor itch of your opinion,
Make yourselves scabs?
(Caius Marcius – Coriolanus)

I had rather had eleven die nobly for their country than one voluptuously
surfeit out of action.
(Volumnia)

You would be another Penelope; yet, they say, all the yarn she spun in
Ulysses' absence did but fill Ithaca full of moths.
(Valeria)

Nature teaches beasts to know their friends.
(Sicinius)

Ingratitude is monstrous.
(Third Citizen)

In soothing them, we nourish 'gainst our Senate
The cockle of rebellion, insolence, sedition,
Which we ourselves have ploughed for, sowed, and scattered,
By mingling them with us, the honoured number.
(Coriolanus)

What is the city but the people?
(Sicinius)

This tiger-footed rage.
(Menenius)

I would you had put your power well on,
Before you had worn it out.
(Volumnia)

You are too absolute.
(Volumnia)

You common cry of curs, whose breath I hate
As reek of the rotten fens, whose loves I prize
As the dead carcasses of unburied men
That do corrupt my air, I banish you…
There is a world elsewhere.
(Coriolanus)

I shall be loved when I am lacked.
(Coriolanus)

I have heard it said the fittest time to corrupt a man's wife is when she's
fall'n out with her husband.
(Roman)

This peace is nothing but to rust iron, increase tailors, and breed ballad-
makers.
(Second Servingman)

I think he'll be to Rome
As is the osprey to the fish, who takes it
By sovereignty of nature.
(Aufidius)

My mother bows,
As if Olympus to a molehill should
In supplication nod.
(Coriolanus)

The noble sister of Pubicola,
The moon of Rome, chaste as the icicle
That's curdied by the frost from purest snow
And hangs on Dian's temple – dear Valeria!
(Coriolanus)

There is no more mercy in him than there is milk in a male tiger.
(Menenius)

At a few drops of women's rheum, which are
As cheap as lies, he sold the blood and labour
Of our great action.
(Aufidius)

MUCH ADO ABOUT NOTHING

It would seem that it is not compulsory for a politician to have a sense of humour: Margaret Thatcher, for example, notoriously failed to have one. Yet, I would suggest, that a sense of humour is a valuable asset for any politician and almost a necessary safety valve (at times perhaps a palladium) when times are dire and grim and the outlook is bleak. And witty ripostes are invaluable at Prime Minister's Question Time. These are the main reasons for a politician to see *Much Ado About Nothing*: it is Shakespeare's funniest play, and much of the humour comes from the wit-filled exchanges between Beatrice and Benedick.

Laughter, of course, is good for all of us, and in addition this play explores so many other relevant themes: deceit and trustworthiness (you can hardly believe a word anyone says); honour and its complex obligations; barefaced villainy; the strange workings of justice and the law; and, strongest of all, the emotional complexity of real love as we witness both sexes self-protecting and fearing commitment.

There are two storylines in *Much Ado About Nothing*. In the main plot Claudio, in the service of Don Pedro, Prince of Aragon, falls in love with Hero, daughter of Leonato, the Governor of Messina, and a marriage is joyously arranged. But Don Pedro's bastard brother, Don John, through a trick which deceives Claudio into thinking that Hero kissed another man at a window at midnight, destroys Claudio's faith in his bride-to-be and he denounces her infidelity at the marriage service, rejecting her. To deflect criticisms of his daughter's behaviour Leonato announces that Hero has died, only for her to come alive again and the marriage happily to be celebrated after the watch, led by the apparently incompetent constable Dogberry, uncover the trickery and villainy that has taken place.

The above story appeared in many versions at the time, though Shakespeare may have taken it from Ariosto. No matter. The subplot – though it is, I think, the most remembered aspect of the play – concerns Beatrice and Benedick. Beatrice is Hero's cousin and Benedick is Claudio's close friend. For most of *Much Ado About Nothing* Beatrice and Benedick engage in battle of witty repartee, superficially indicating the scorn each has for the other but in fact concealing a mutual attraction and love (which is revealed through tricks played by their friends.) After Claudio's cruel rejection of her cousin, Beatrice demands that Benedick show his love for her by killing him. He reluctantly challenges his friend Claudio to a duel, though the discovery of Don John's villainy ensures there is no confrontation. Beatrice and Benedick too marry.

Those are the plots, perhaps in themselves not exceptional – but let us see how Shakespeare handles the themes of *Much Ado About Nothing*.

First of all, deceit and disguise. There is the disguise of the mutual affection between Beatrice and Benedick hidden behind their rifle-shot banter of mutual dismissal and scorn, which I will look at later. And there is the obvious deceit and treachery of Don John as he undermines Claudio's love for Hero by verbal insinuation and physical deception. These are the obvious instances of false appearances which both conceal and confuse. The play, though, is in fact riddled with disguise and tricks.

Claudio is smitten with love (for Hero) for apparently the first time in his young and inexperienced life and so the more worldly Don Pedro undertakes to woo Hero on his behalf – to which end all the young men confront the ladies as masquers in Act 2 Scene 1. At the end of the play, with Claudio believing Hero dead and agreeing to marry her cousin, the ladies are brought forward, masked. Masques conceal reality: nothing is straightforward! In between the masked scenes we have the deceit of Don Pedro, Claudio and Leonato, knowing that Benedick is listening, saying how much – "with an enraged affection" – Beatrice loves Benedick but will die before admitting it, and the parallel scene of Hero and Ursula, with Beatrice hidden, extolling Benedick's virtues and how he is wasting away for love of the scornful Beatrice. People are playing tricks on each other all the time. It all, very effectively, adds to the humour but all certainties are palpably undermined.

There is a lovely song in the play with the repeated memorable line "Men were deceivers ever." It is not just men, though, but women and beauty too which are agents of deception. Hero is seen to be a very worthy young woman at the outset of *Much Ado About Nothing* but, on Claudio's denouncement of her as a "rotten orange" and an "approved wanton", her own father is quick to believe the Princes and Claudio and reject her. It's all to do with beauty and the effect beauty is believed to have on men: friendship goes out of the window when a woman and love get between friends. Men are not the only sex that are deceivers ever. In fact the biggest deception of all is the pretence that Hero has died after being rejected by Claudio. It leads to happy endings all round but we know that in Messina, the setting of the play, we can never be sure that things are as they seem[10] or will continue so.

Honour is an aspect of *Much Ado About Nothing* that I want to look at now. As we shall see it is a theme that runs through so many of Shakespeare's plays. It is defined by Norman Council, in his book *When Honour's at the Stake*, dealing with just this question, as "the reward due to virtuous action" and therefore links very closely with one's reputation. In *Much Ado About Nothing* once Hero is believed to have had premarital sex with Borachio she has lost her honour and her reputation; her father Leonato consequently immediately rejects her for having "fallen into a pit of ink". He too feels his honour destroyed and wishes he were dead.

Once Leonato, though, has heard the Friar and Benedick express their belief in his daughter being guiltless – that the accusers have "wronged her honour" – he, despite his age, challenges Claudio to a duel. The strongest obligation to avenge Hero's honour is, however, placed on Benedick: when Benedick tells Beatrice that he will do anything for her, her chilling response is "Kill Claudio." Everything is resolved before any duels take place but the point is that an old man is prepared to die to avenge the slander of his daughter's reputation and (although there is also, admittedly, a strong element of proving

10   We also find this in *A Midsummer Night's Dream*, *The Merchant of Venice*, *Twelfth Night*, *As You Like It*, *Pericles*, *The Winter's Tale* etc.

his love for Beatrice in his behaviour) Benedick, initially reluctantly, is prepared to put close friendship aside and fight (and kill) Claudio for his traducing of Hero. (It is noteworthy, though, that Leonato is prepared to bend the strict letter of the "no sex before marriage" law if Hero's transgression had been with her husband-to-be in response to his importuning.)

Honour is a significant concept in Shakespeare's plays. I tend to think that it is more honoured in the breach than the observance in the 21st century.

The perpetrator of the villainy in *Much Ado About Nothing* is Don John, the Bastard, but even though the perpetrator of the villainy in the subplot of *King Lear* is Edmund, Gloucester's son who is also a bastard, I don't think Shakespeare is intent on branding all bastards as villains.[11] After all the biggest villain of all is Iago in *Othello* and there are no doubts cast on his paternity. Even though Shakespeare's villains frequently enjoy committing evil for the sheer devilment of it, there are psychological reasons too to be found for their behaviour. We hear early in the play that Don John has recently been reconciled to the Prince, his brother. But, it would appear, not sufficiently closely reconciled, as he is envious of "that young upstart" Claudio who has become his brother's right-hand man – a position Don John covets as it once was his. Therefore creating disharmony between Don Pedro and Claudio cannot but redound to Don John's advantage. Such is the feeling of displeasure that the taciturn Don John has towards Claudio that he claims he will do anything to show his contempt and offers Borachio a thousand ducats for the implementation of his plan to discredit and destroy Hero and thus humiliate Claudio. I find it interesting that, although in the Elizabethan world the bastardy of Don John would immediately signify evil (their begetting had flouted the necessary law and order signified by marriage), Shakespeare is not content with formulaic villains and gives us, however briefly, genuine personal motives for Don John's conduct.

Villainy. Not everyone has the purest of motives. "…one may smile,

11   The two other real bastards in Shakespeare's plays are Thersites in *Troilus and Cressida* and Philip Faulconbridge in *King John*, the latter being an exception to the bastards are villains guideline.

and smile, and be a villain". (Hamlet)

Before concluding with what the Beatrice/Benedick love theme has to say to us, I want to consider Dogberry and the Watch. Dogberry provides verbal amusement[12] and an expressed belief about the law and its operations which would seem to lead to the avoidance of any arrests, and yet it is in fact the Watch that apprehends the malefactors and sees to it that justice is done. In the first instance Dogberry seems to enjoy the sound of words without being particular about their meaning: he confuses 'damnation' with 'salvation', 'sensible' with 'senseless', 'odorous' with 'odious', 'opinioned' with 'pinioned' and so on – his influence even extends to the second watchman who invokes 'lechery' when he means 'treachery'. These are not so much malapropisms as mirrors in sound of the intended words. And Dogberry's insistence that the Watch should not offend anyone when carrying out their duties, a policy of inoffensive inactivity, is contrary to any police policy everywhere in the world, one would think! Yet, in the world of deception and overhearing that *Much Ado About Nothing* inhabits, the Watch is successful, makes the appropriate arrests and ensures a happy ending. On one level Dogberry's fumbling with words is an apposite counterpoint to the shimmering brilliance of Beatrice and Benedick's word-jousting and on another level his bumbling incompetence, preaching inactivity, is contrasted with the clever activity of Don John who seeks "any model to build mischief on". Yet what fundamentally comes across from Dogberry and his companions' antics is the affection felt for them by Shakespeare and his seeing their well-meaning, a quality which is far from exclusive to the lords and ladies who constitute the main plots. You could not claim that Shakespeare is a socialist

12. In the film of *Much Ado About Nothing*, directed by Kenneth Branagh, who also played Benedick to Emma Thompson's Beatrice, Dogberry and Vosges are disastrously played by Michael Keaton and Ben Elton respectively. Their whole focus is on physical slapstick and the humour in Dogberry's words is lost completely. The film (made in Tuscany) is scenically ravishing which I think distracts from Shakespeare's presentation of the Beatrice/Benedick theme right at the start of the play. Branagh and Thompson do pretty well as the would-not-be lovers, but I remember very fondly Judi Dench and Donald Sinden in the roles with the Royal Shakespeare Company in 1976.

on the evidence of this play but neither could you claim that he is a snob. It's not just the rich and the nobility who have the answers – ordinary folks do too, even if they come at them by unexpected routes!

Finally we come to Beatrice and Benedick, not known as lovers in the way that Romeo and Juliet, Antony and Cleopatra, Hero and Leander, Troilus and Cressida, Dante and Beatrice et al. are known: there is a contrariness about their encounters but they are the only pair for whom there is finally a joyous coming together in this life, although there is an acknowledgment that "thou and I are too wise to woo peaceably". Those are Benedick's words but it is Beatrice who has the last say in their verbal jousting when she professes to yield to Benedick reluctantly and "to save your life, for I was told you were in a consumption". Benedick then silences her with the only means apparently possible – a kiss – and the play concludes with Benedick insisting on dancing and extolling marriage as a panacea for sadness.

It has not always been thus between them. From Beatrice we know they have some history together, that Benedick won her heart "with false dice". And from the beginning of *Much Ado About Nothing* she is determined to disparage him, which we can see as a kind of protective defence mechanism to ensure that he will never wound her again. Her uncle, Leonato, talks of "a merry war betwixt Signor Benedick and her; they never meet but there's a skirmish of wit between them". This skirmish is fun for those who witness it in the play and also for us, the audience. For example, this is their first encounter:

> *Beatrice: I wonder that you will still be talking, Signor Benedick, nobody marks you.*
> *Benedick: What, my dear Lady Disdain, Are you yet living?*

But even before this encounter Beatrice has expressed an interest in the fate of Benedick on his return from the wars: indeed her first words are an enquiry about him, albeit expressed in terms of disparagement. Benedick immediately establishes himself as a ladies' man: "it is certain I am loved of all ladies, only you excepted". They have been close enough to address each other directly, eye-to-eye, no flinching. There is no doubt of the strength of their mutual feeling.

They share too a common attitude towards (love and) marriage. Beatrice avers that "I had rather hear my dog bark at a crow than a man swear he loves me." She is on her knees morning and night asking God not to send her a husband, and when she dies a virgin she wishes for herself a place amongst the unmarried men and women. For his part Benedick, talking of Beatrice's words stabbing him as though they were daggers, is initially determined not to marry Beatrice "though she were endowed with all that Adam had left him before he transgressed". Later he affirms that "till all graces be in one woman, one woman shall not come in my grace". It could be argued that each protests too much, that underlying their apparent hostility is a fear of commitment and loss of individuality and that these protestations themselves, with all their vehemence, denote the compulsive attraction that each is trying to fend off.

What is also apparent – in contrast to what is seen as the unthinking love of the young Hero and Claudio – is that there is a certain cynicism about marriage pervading Messina. There are numerous references to married men (almost) inevitably acquiring cuckold's horns through their wife's infidelity. Peace of mind does not come with marriage: as Don John says, "What is he for a fool that betrothes himself to unquietness?" All this emphasises the strong male fear of the power that women ultimately hold in relationships.[13] I think the reality of the power women hold is also seen in *Much Ado About Nothing* in that Beatrice appears to have the upper hand over Benedick. Benedick is the more ready to submit to the idea of marriage to Beatrice, admitting that "I have railed so long against marriage", but then justifying his new-found position with: "...doth not the appetite alter? A man loves the meat in his youth that he cannot endure in his age." Though, in truth, overhearing herself condemned for scorn and pride and Hero extolling the almost incomparable virtues of Benedick, Beatrice very quickly is prepared to requite Benedick by marrying him. The whole feel of marriage, though, in Messina is that it is men who ultimately have more to lose and that women by their wiles and sexual infidelity bring stress

13   *The Taming of the Shrew* also provides an interesting commentary on the power play between men and women in a relationship.

to their husbands.

Which means that at the end of *Much Ado About Nothing*, although Benedick appears beside himself with happiness we wonder how long that feeling will last. That is one thing to talk about from the play, as is the whole nature of the fear of commitment and self-protection in relationships, which that of Beatrice and Benedick exhibits. One of the joys of Shakespeare is that he opens up so many issues without himself making judgments. As we have seen *Much Ado About Nothing* takes us also into the realms of pretence and deceit, honour and reputation, villainy and the strange workings of justice. There are a number of references to fashion and how it changes and some human comments about war too. When you see the play you will hear them. Maybe there are flaws in the play – for example the character of Claudio is not very likeable and the Borachio/Margaret window scene could easily have been rumbled by Margaret herself, or indeed Beatrice, one would have thought. But *Much Ado About Nothing* is fundamentally a witty and joyous play, but as with all Shakespeare's plays, it is grounded in the real psychological complexities and recognisable humanity of us all. We leave the theatre better, wiser – and warm inside.

Memorable Quotations From *Much Ado About Nothing*

I had rather hear my dog bark at a crow than a man swear he loves me.
(Beatrice)

He that hath a beard is more than a youth, and he that hath no beard is less than a man.
(Beatrice)

Friendship is a constant in all other things
Save in the office and affairs of love.
(Claudio)

Time goes on crutches till love have all his rites.
(Claudio)

Is it not strange that sheep's guts should hale souls out of men's bodies?
(Benedick)

Men were deceivers ever.
(Balthasar)

But doth not the appetite alter? A man loves the meat in his youth that he cannot endure in his age.
(Benedick)

Well, everyone can master a grief but he that hath it.
(Benedick)

...they that touch pitch will be defiled.
(Dogberry)

For when rich villains have need of poor ones, poor ones may make what price they will.
(Borachio)

…the fashions wear out more apparel than the man.
(Conrade)

When the age is in, the wit is out.
(Dogberry)

…an two men ride of a horse, one must ride behind.
(Dogberry)

…a word in your ear.
(Dogberry)

For there was never yet philosopher
That could endure the toothache patiently.
(Leonato)

I was not born under a rhyming planet, nor I cannot woo in festival terms.
(Benedick)

KING LEAR

After watching a somewhat eccentric production of Seneca's *Thyestes* I was talking in the ADC Theatre Cambridge bar with my son (who had played the title role in *Thyestes*) and his friends and mentioned that my favourite Shakespeare plays were *King Lear* and *Antony and Cleopatra*[14]. There was some surprise that I had not mentioned *Hamlet*. Perhaps many years ago I would have opted for *Hamlet* – and I do love the play – but it is a young man's play, an Oedipal son coming to terms with his father's death and his mother's marriage to his father's murderer. A pretty powerful and seminally Freudian human situation, but it does not cover the wide range of themes explored in *King Lear*.

King Lear is concerned with the fear and weaknesses of old age; it is concerned with madness – the fear of which is not confined to old age; it, like *Hamlet*, is concerned with the parent/child relationship; it contains a savage commentary on social injustice; it works towards what I believe is a theme which deserves to be central in all human relationships – reconciliation and forgiveness; and it is also about uses and abuses of power and the appropriate surrendering of power. This last theme is the trigger of all subsequent action in *King Lear*, and there is speculation that our current Queen, having seen *King Lear*, has her reluctance to surrender her throne to her son endorsed and fears his banishment of her to a council estate in Leicester – à la Sue Townsend.

The main story of the play is simple. King Lear, at the age of eighty, determines to divide his kingdom into three, to be ruled over by

---

14   My love of *Antony and Cleopatra* maybe needs some explanation. Two things endear the play to me: the exquisite level of the verse and the character of Cleopatra, and I would like now to add *Othello* to my pantheon of favourite plays.

his three daughters and their husbands. He will keep a retinue of a hundred knights and will, freed from the cares of state, visit his daughters in turn. He has reserved the best portion of his kingdom for his youngest and favourite daughter Cordelia, but when she fails to express her unreserved love for him Lear, in a fit of rage, banishes her and, undowried, she marries the King of France and leaves the kingdom. Lear's other two daughters, Goneril and Regan, who have previously been ultra-effusive in their love for their father, now plot against him, denying him any retinue. Lear then chooses to be outdoors at the mercy of the elements. He is accompanied by his Fool, by a disguised Kent (previously banished for speaking up on behalf of Cordelia) and by Edgar (see next paragraph) as Mad Tom. Lear is never far from madness. Eventually Cordelia returns to right the wrongs suffered by her father and there is forgiveness and reconciliation before both die, Cordelia hanged and her father's heart giving way.

There is a subplot concerning the Duke of Gloucester's two sons, the legitimate Edgar and the bastard Edmund. Edmund so discredits his brother that Edgar has to flee in disguise. Edmund reveals to Regan and her husband that his father has been corresponding with Cordelia and a potential French invasion. As a punishment Gloucester is blinded and thrown outdoors and left to roam and to meet Lear, two powerless old men, rejected by their children. Edmund is ruthless for power and flirts with both Goneril and Regan to further this end. Finally he is killed in a duel by Edgar, and Edgar, Kent and Albany (Goneril's weak but decent husband) are left to patch up the pieces of a shattered realm. (Gloucester, Goneril and Regan, and Lear's Fool also having died.)

Let us first consider the theme of old age. Today's general consensus is that the two most evident concomitants of old age are incontinence and paranoia. There is absolutely no evidence within the play for Lear being incontinent – he is wet through in the storm scene on the heath but it is an external force rather than an internal lack of control which brings this about. As for paranoia, if we mean the contemporary use of it as an abnormal tendency to be suspicious of and distrust others, it could be argued that his ongoing experiences in the play give him every reason for distrusting others, his elder daughters in particular. But if we use paranoia in its age-old sense of a mental derangement characterized by delusions and hallucinations then certainly the word fits. In the storm on the heath he hallucinates the dogs Tray, Blanch and Sweetheart for example, and there is the sweetest and saddest of all delusions when he dies of joy believing that Cordelia may be alive.

That Lear is old is indisputable. At the outset of *King Lear* he expresses his wish to "unburthen'd crawl towards death". He is shedding himself of his responsibilities, hoping for a quiet ending. Regan talks of his natural life having just about reached its limit. It is Regan too who complains that Lear held on to his powers too long. In fact it is always Regan who is most incisive vis-à-vis comments on Lear's age. She it is who says that "as you are old and reverend, should be wise", and who says tellingly to her sister earlier that "he hath but slenderly known himself". And this latter statement seems to me to be the crux of the play. There is always the hope that old age brings wisdom or at the very least a certain learning which can offset the body's increasing uselessness. Self-knowledge is a desirable aim and the importunate Lear, demanding extravagant verbal bouquets of love from his daughters, has to go through both meteorological and mental storms of devastating anguish before he can admit to being "a very foolish fond old man" and before he can ask Cordelia to forgive and forget. In addition to the acquisition of a certain amount of self-knowledge Lear learns something about court flattery and trust, and about the condition of his poorest subjects.

I will say something about that last aspect a little later but, staying with the theme of old age, what Shakespeare has presented us with is an old man's fall from power (which happens as our age necessitates our relinquishing our work) and a descent into madness (which we all fear). There is a horny old A Level question which quotes Lear; "I am a man more sinned against than sinning" and asks for a discussion thereon. On the evidence of the play itself – as distinct from anything we might surmise that took place before the play opened – there is only one case to be made. Old people should never be treated as is Lear! Even though he has much to learn when the play opens, his age, perhaps despite his regal position, demands respect, care and concern.

How mad is Lear? Arguably his decision to surrender his power at the outset of the play, and especially the way he does it, is an indication of a man not in his perfect mind. Certainly his heartfelt cry at the end of the first Act: "O! let me not be mad, not mad, sweet heaven" echoes in our minds throughout the play. His arraignment of the daughters he sees in his mind's eye, the excesses of his vitriolic invective against Goneril and Regan and his running away from Cordelia's representative at Dover where he admits to being "cut to th' brains" all attest to his lack of sanity. And old people, experiencing almost every day some deterioration of the body, realise that inevitably the same must be happening to the mind.

Take that original decision to distribute his kingdom on the basis of how much love his daughter will profess to him. A daft decision, but comprehensible if we accept an increasing paranoia and a need for love that old people possess. The distribution is based on the trust that he unquestioningly believes exists between a father and his daughters/children: he has a good deal to learn and has to experience a degree of madness before a measure of wisdom is granted. His Fool justifies his calling Lear a fool: "All thy other titles thou hast given away; that / Thou wast born with." Lear himself talks of being born, in tears, and coming "to this great stage of fools" or, as Estragon says in Beckett's *Waiting for Godot*: "We are all born mad. Some remain so."

Of course madness and foolishness are not the same thing. We can all do – and indeed *do* do – foolish things, but it is probably not necessary for us all to go through the suffering of madness in order to achieve a degree of insight and understanding of life in old age. But that fear of madness being just around the corner is a real fear for the elderly – increasingly forgetful, increasingly incapable of staying awake when reading *The Brothers Karamazov*, increasingly beset by disturbing dreams and sleeplessness, it is no wonder that old people see madness as lurking behind the next bend in the road. And Lear wonderfully acts it out for all of us, and achieves peace of mind right at his end.

I have mentioned the present Queen holding on to power, giving no indication of when she may abdicate. I can understand the frustrations of her ageing son, but I do not expect him to behave in a similar manner to Goneril and Regan. But this handing down of power from one generation to the next is not only a matter for monarchs and politicians. It affects us all. The trite, jokey statement about parents spending their children's inheritance encapsulates an important aspect of this situation. Somewhere along the line the elderly have to give way to the young, their children; they downsize from what has been the family home; their financial needs have decreased; their life involves less rushing around, has become much quieter – is it then not right to give the family home to a favoured son or daughter? Should it be shared between siblings, and if a mother or father or both can no longer live on their own, can their children accommodate them? It is a basic, almost banal question, but it is one of the many themes of *King Lear*. And no answers are provided... except that it is foolish to base any decision on flattery!

Perhaps it is equally foolish not to play the game that your father and convention decree: to be scrupulous about the niceties of complete honesty when white lies are clearly demanded. I refer, of course, to Cordelia's self-righteous refusal to countenance stretching the truth about the nature of parental and marital obligations in order to please her father. She did not have to heave her heart into her mouth to do so; just a measure of pretence would have done – the same kind of pretence that is heard daily up and down the land at funeral services. For this lack of complaisance James Agate refers to "the gormless Cordelia". All this is true but obviously without Cordelia's paint-stripper honesty the plot of *King Lear*, with its madness and horrors and duplicity and reconciliation, would never have got off the ground.

I am not suggesting that Cordelia's shortcomings begin to equate with those of Goneril and Regan. Her offence is one of disingenuous honesty; theirs is one of deceit and deliberate malfeasance. Today we consign our aged parents to an old people's home, some of which are comfortable havens; we do not effectively banish them to fend for themselves outdoors at the mercy of the elements and whatever might befall. But perhaps what the elderly really want is the protection and love of their children – certainly this is what Lear expects. When this is denied him, his rage against their inhospitality is excessive and, as I have argued previously, indicates his unhingement. He calls his daughters "unnatural hags"; he asks for lightning to blind Regan and for her beauty to be infected and blistered. Most powerfully of all he calls upon the Goddess Nature to convey sterility into Goneril's womb and, if this cannot happen, to ensure that any child she has will be a "disnatur'd torment to her", mock her and make her prematurely old. At the end of this last speech Lear utters the definitive words on the subject of father/child relationships: he wishes Goneril to feel "How sharper than a serpent's tooth it is / To have a thankless child!"

And therein lies the crux of *King Lear*, the pivot around which the whole play turns. It accounts for the old father Lear's excesses of vituperation against his daughters. Many societies treat the old with care and respect; we don't. Lear, Goneril, Regan and Cordelia (and Gloucester, Edmund and Edgar) are manifestly exaggerated or extreme examples of parent/child discord and the consequent appalling treatment of the fathers, but as such, archetypes if you like, they speak to us, touch nerves and ask us to examine over and over our relationship with our parents. Personally I think parents have to earn the love and respect of their children; I do not believe that it should be given automatically. But I know personally the joy I feel when I have experienced the love of my children or when one of them says (s)he has enjoyed something I have written (and I imagine this line of communication runs both ways). I also know of the fear of parental rejection, which frequently results in a parent egg-shelling around on tiptoe in case the wrath of a child suddenly erupts. And there are so many cases after divorce and a second marriage when an incompatibility between the new wife and daughter (in my experience it is almost always two females rather than two males who experience the incompatibility) has led to the wife demanding her new husband choosing between herself and his daughter(s). My second wife has always insisted that my children come first, and I think she is right. But Lear's children usurped the natural order of things; with scant, or no, regard for their father, they prioritised their greed above everything else. *King Lear* provides us with an opportunity to open up a discussion on parent/child relationships and thereby to establish what are the fundamentals and most important aspects of such relationships.

There are strong political and social aspects of *King Lear* too. I want to focus on the social aspects but just want to mention *en passant* the offering of sexual favours to Edmund by both Goneril and Regan and Edmund's ruthless exploitation of them both (in addition to the destruction of his father) in his attempt to gain power. With Edmund the lust for power is not overtly for political purposes; it is probably more a compensatory mechanism for his having been born a bastard and hence made to feel inferior. But denunciation of parents was a power tool used by a civilised nation less than a hundred years ago and sleeping your way to the top (though usually by women) has certainly not gone out of fashion. The lure of power is no respecter of common decency or conventional morality.

Lear's descent into madness is also a descent into living the life of a "poor naked wretch", enabling him to experience life as one of his poorest subjects. His railings against sex/copulation and women – "down from the waist they are Centaurs... / But to the girdle do the Gods inherit, / Beneath is all the fiend's" is a direct response to his treatment by his daughters, whereas his social insights stem from being taken away from a life of court intrigue and gossip and "scurvy politicians" and confronted with the necessity of everyday survival.

I have argued elsewhere[15] about the need for politicians (or those in authority) to constantly remind themselves of their common humanity, perhaps especially at a time of economic difficulties when politicians prioritise the needs of the 'nation' over the needs of the people who make up the nation. In *King Lear* the old King realises the nature of power and authority: "A dog's obeyed in office" and how the rich can cover up their sins in a way that the poor cannot afford: "Through tater'd clothes small vices appear; / Robes and furr'd gowns hide all." At a time when any small-fry benefit scrounger is demonised, whereas the avoidance of paying tax, which is the acknowledged way of expressing one's responsibility to the community, is praised almost as an art form, it is salutary to hear Lear's understanding that gold buys, and therefore perverts, justice. So often in both the UK and the USA court decisions are based on who is able to pay for the best lawyer.

Through his experiences Lear begins to understand what it is to be human, to be unaccommodated, without the trappings of civilization:

15   In my book *Novels for Ed.* (Grosvenor House Publishing Ltd., February 2012)

for, one suspects, the first time in his life he understands basic human needs and has some compassion for his poorest subjects. In 1971 the Russian director Grigori Kozintsev made a powerful and provocative film of *King Lear* (*Korol Lir*)[16], with script by Pasternak and music by Shostakovich, in which he emphasized the poverty of Lear's Britain with packs of displaced beggars constantly around. It was a socialist perspective on *King Lear* but a visual echoing of Lear's own ultimate perception.

There are other themes in *King Lear* but none so important as those we have just looked at. As far as characterisation is concerned we have mentioned the initial foolishness of Cordelia and, although their behaviour in this play is completely reprehensible, Lear's previous reluctance to step down from power does give Goneril and Regan motivation. The point being is that in almost all of his plays Shakespeare does not deal with extremes of black and white. Both Gloucester and Edgar, who represent that which is noble and loyal, are guilty of credulity and gullibility. Even Edmund, admittedly at the point of death, attempts to do some good "despite of mine own nature" by attempting to save the lives of Lear and Cordelia whose deaths he had previous sanctioned. So it goes on – Kent behaves rashly, Albany weakly. But I must confess I can find no fault in the character of the Fool…

Edmund in his early speech rejects astrology as a cop-out – "we make guilty of our disasters the sun, the moon, and stars"; it is an excuse for refusing to take personal responsibility. He also introduces the question of human nature and its apparently being governed by self-interest, by greed, cruelty and lust. The world of *King Lear* at the beginning is a pagan world of extreme wealth and extreme poverty, almost a Tennysonian world of "nature, red in tooth and

16   Amongst various film versions of *King Lear* there is an interesting parallel version, based on a contemporary novel by Jane Smiley. The film (1997) and novel both go by the title of *A Thousand Acres*. Despite the efforts of Jessica Lange (as Ginny), Michelle Pfeiffer (as Rose) and Jennifer Jason Leigh (as Caroline), and with Jason Robards and Colin Firth, the film, unlike the novel, is something of a turkey. Jane Smiley accounts for Ginny and Rose being so hostile to their father: sexual abuse as teenagers being the reason – interesting but not an iota of evidence for this in Shakespeare's play.

claw". Lear, on the blasted heath, learns, like Vladimir and Estragon in *Waiting for Godot*, the basic qualities we need to survive – patience and fortitude.

But survival is not where it ends. What Lear has also learned by the end of the play is that love and forgiveness are at the heart of being human. (Even Edmund accesses a glimmer of this truth.) So there has been a progress from a world of pagan values to a world of Christian values. And there has been reconciliation (Lear and Cordelia essentially, but also Edgar and Edmund) and some sort of restoration of order.

Love, forgiveness, reconciliation, restoration of order – these are paramount Shakespearean themes, appearing again and again throughout his plays. It is a very uneasy order that is restored in *King Lear* with Edgar, who has played the idiot savant so convincingly, entrusted by Albany to "rule in this realm". But there is no dispute over the qualities of love, forgiveness and reconciliation that remain with us after the horrors we have witnessed – horrors that also, salutarily, stay with us.

I don't believe it necessary for us all to go on a personal journey of discovery and experience the madness and squalour and faithlessness that Lear does. He is the archetype that does it for us, that represents mankind. We may not identify with Lear the king, but when reduced to his essentials as an "unaccommodated man… a poor, bare forked animal", we identify with Lear the representative of the human race. And we share his insights and understanding: insights and understanding about the nature of human needs, about the power of the rich and the weaknesses of the poor, about injustice, about the fear of madness, about the need for love within families, about forgiveness and reconciliation – about compassion.

I think *King Lear* is breathtaking in its wisdom. A great play.

Memorable Quotations From *King Lear*

Nothing will come of nothing.
(Lear)

Come not between the dragon and his wrath.
(Lear)

'Tis the infirmity of his age; yet he hath ever but slenderly known himself.
(Regan)

Now, gods, stand up for bastards!
(Edmund)

We have seen the best of our time.
(Gloucester)

Dost thou call me fool, boy?
(Lear)
All thy other titles thou hast given away; that thou wast born with.
(Fool)

As you are old and reverend, should be wise.
(Goneril)

How sharper than a serpent's tooth it is
To have a thankless child!
(Lear)

Thou should'st not have been old till thou hadst been wise.
(Fool)
O! let me not be mad, not mad, sweet heaven!
(Lear)

Why, Madam, if I were your father's dog,
You should not use me so.
(Kent)

Winter's not gone yet, if the wild-geese fly that way.
(Fool)

O, Sir! you are old;
Nature in you stands on the very verge
Of her confine.
(Regan)

I pray you, father, being weak, seem so.
(Regan)

O! reason not the need; our basest beggars
Are in the poorest thing superfluous:
Allow not nature more than nature needs,
Man's life is cheap as beast's.
(Lear)

I tax not you, you elements with unkindness;
I never gave you kingdom, call'd you children,
You owe me no subscription.
(Lear)

For there was never yet fair woman but she made mouths in a glass.
(Fool)

I am a man more sinn'd against than sinning.
(Lear)

The younger rises when the old doth fall.
(Edmund)

Take physic, Pomp;
Expose thyself to feel what wretches feel.
(Lear)

43

...'twas this flesh begot those pelican daughters.
(Lear)

...thou art the thing itself; unaccommodated man is no more but such a poor, bare, forked animal as thou art.
(Lear)

...'tis a naughty night to swim in.
(Fool)

He's mad that trusts in the tameness of a wolf, a horse's health, a boy's love, or a whore's oath.
(Fool)

As flies to wanton boys, are we to th' Gods;
They kill us for their sport.
(Gloucester)

I have been worth the whistle.
(Goneril)

Why I do trifle thus with his despair
Is done to cure it.
(Edgar)

Ay, every inch a king.
(Lear)

There thou migh'st behold
The great image of Authority:
A dog's obey'd in office.
(Lear)

Thorough tatter'd clothes small vices appear;
Robes and furr'd gowns hide all.
(Lear)

When we are born we cry that we are come
To this great stage of fools.
(Lear)

Pray, do not mock me:
I am a very foolish, fond old man.
(Lear)

Men must endure
Their going hence, even as their coming hither:
Ripeness is all.
(Edgar)

We two alone will sing like birds i' the cage
(Lear)

Jesters do oft prove prophets.
(Regan)

The Gods are just, and of our pleasant vices
Make instruments to plague us.
(Edgar)

The wheel is come full circle.
(Edmund)

Never, never, never, never, never!
(Lear)

The oldest hath borne most: we that are young
Shall never see so much, nor live so long.
(Edgar)

PERICLES

In the first part of the 17th century *Pericles* was one of Shakespeare's most frequently performed plays.[17] Today it is far less popular. I have seen it twice only: once quite recently at the Globe (2005) and once, memorably, at Stratford in 1969. This latter was directed by Terry Hands; the set was bare apart from the backdrop of an enlarged, and therefore dominating, reproduction of da Vinci's *Vetruvian Man*. Appropriately this symbolises the correlation of ideal human proportions; a kind of harmony, balance and idealism which *Pericles* ultimately represents. It was, though, the performance of Ian Richardson as Pericles that I remember most vividly. His voice. Melodious and harmonious, totally responsive to the rhythm of the verse, Richardson's voice was completely attuned to the mood of the play.

By mood I am referring to the inevitable ultimate reconciliations of the play. Hellish things happen to Pericles, Marina and Thaisa in the course of *Pericles* but we know from the opening words of Gower (as Chorus) that all will end well – he talks of the story we are about to see enacted as a time-honoured "restorative" whose purpose is to "make men glorious". Bringing families together is a common conclusion to so many of Shakespeare's comedies and late plays – *As You Like It* and *The Winter's Tale* for example – and indeed we find the same theme in Shakespeare's first play *The Comedy of Errors*, but nowhere is this harmonious conclusion stronger and more uplifting than it is in *Pericles*.

Not that I am recommending this play simply because it has an almost unbearable happy ending. In addition to the ending we have treachery, betrayal, incest, the ravages of fortune, lust, envy and theories of government among the topics raised and discussed in

17   *Pericles* was very popular until the closure of the theatres in 1642.

Pericles. Important themes for all of us, and certainly for politicians. But more of those later; let me now clarify the storyline of the play.

The play starts with Pericles in Antioch as a suitor for Antiochus' daughter: to win her he has to solve a riddle, which he does, but in doing so imperils his life. Knowing his life in his state of Tyre to be unsafe he takes to the high seas, leaving Helicanus to govern in Tyre. However he is shipwrecked and thrown ashore in Pentapolis where, in a tournament, he wins the hand of the King's daughter, Thaisa. They set sail for Tyre together, but a storm at sea causes the apparent death of Thaisa, having given birth to Marina: Thaisa is coffined and consigned to the sea and Pericles entrusts Marina to the care of Cleon, governor of Tarsus. We also learn that Thaisa has miraculously survived and, believing her husband to be dead, has become a priestess at the temple of Diana in Ephesus.

Sixteen years then elapse, with Pericles in Tyre and Marina in Tarsus and Thaisa in Ephesus. Such is the grace and beauty of Marina that she eclipses Cleon's own similarly aged daughter and so Cleon decrees that she be killed. Just before this happens, however, she is captured by pirates and sold to a brothel in Mytilene. Marina's transparent purity saves her from being debauched. At sea again and distraught by the perceived death of Marina, Pericles sails to Mytilene and, in arguably the most moving moment in the history of theatre, recognizes and is reunited with Marina. Then in a vision the goddess Diana directs Pericles to Ephesus where he is reunited with Thaisa. Lysimachus, the governor of Mytilene, who rescued Marina from the brothel, marries Marina and he and Marina are set to rule in Tyre while Pericles and Thaisa will rule in Pentapolis. All resolved, all happy – after heartache upon heartache.

It is difficult to find character flaws in Pericles: his unkempt appearance in sackcloth and uncut hair are natural responses to the extreme personal injuries by which he has been beset, and otherwise he seems intelligent, loving and a thoughtful ruler. It is even more difficult to find character flaws in Marina: she outshines everyone in beauty, skills and virtue. But to see these two as individualised characters is to miss the point. They are, in essence, archetypes, representatives of all that is good in mankind. They make their journey – "thwarting the wayward seas" - through life on our behalf. They meet disaster after disaster and unlike Shakespeare's tragic heroes this is through no fault of their own, no personal character defects. They are Everyman, you and me. Of course it is extremely unlikely that the fate of you and me will be as extreme as that experienced by Pericles and Marina: running for one's life and losing one's wife and daughter on the one hand, and landing up in a brothel with our virginity being auctioned to the highest bidder on the other. But life does deal us all blows, frequently undeserved – government mismanagement of the economy causing mass unemployment for example. Shakespeare, through Pericles and Marina, demonstrates that a kind of excellence and virtue – an ultimate generosity of spirit – are qualities to be cultivated; qualities which can ensure survival.

This, I think, is especially true in the case of Marina. No one doubts her skills: we hear of her weaving and needlework accomplishments, her musical talents, her writing abilities for which she gets "all praises" – all of which put Cleon's daughter Philoten in the shade and which thence lead Cleon to arrange her murder. And no one essays any adverse comment about her character: even the Bawd in the brothel admits that were the devil to so much beg a kiss of her she "would make a puritan" of him. The man that Marina is ultimately to marry, Lycurgus, the Governor of Mytilene, sees her as "a piece of virtue" and asserts: "Had I brought hither a corrupted mind,[18] / Thy speech had altered it."

Thaisa is a pretty faultless character too, but I am focusing on Pericles and Marina for this is what Shakespeare does. Yes, the love between husband and wife is celebrated[19] and exalted, but even more so is that between father and daughter. We encounter fathers protective of their daughters in Shakespeare's plays – Egeus of Hermia in *A Midsummer Night's Dream* and Prospero of Miranda in *The Tempest*; we encounter fathers with fraught relationships with their daughters – Lear with Goneril, Regan and Cordelia in *King Lear*. (Mother/ son relationships are, of course, examined too – as we have seen

18   Marina's future husband, Lycurgus, met her in the brothel. If his mind was not corrupted why was he there in the first place? Maybe I am being a little sanctimonious, but is he really a suitable husband for Marina?

19   It is in *The Winter's Tale* that we have a similar restoration of a husband and wife, Leontes and Hermione.

in *Coriolanus* and will see at their most dynamic in *Hamlet*.) But the Pericles/Marina relationship is a very special one. Cynics will say that their having spent so little time together accounts for the idealistic nature of their relationship, which is based simply on their shared joy at discovering each other again after fifteen years and after all their travails. But, as ever, cynics miss the point. *Pericles* is an archetypal human mystery tour, with mankind in the hands of the gods, a journey that is resolved with an acceptable happy and moral ending. It serves as a template for what might and could be. In its presentation of Pericles and Marina *Pericles* is idealistic, but this idealism is contrasted with the unpleasantness of the real world of Antioch, where we have a long-standing incestuous father/daughter relationship which with "long use [was]] accounted no sin". This is the world Pericles enters at the start of the play and from which he has to flee for his life. It makes a startling contrast to the Pericles/Marina relationship.

And there *is* a real world in *Pericles*. Not only is there Antioch, a city of incestuous sin with a king organizing the death of anyone who either failed or succeeded in solving the incest riddle, but there is also Tharsus, where there is a massive food shortage: "So sharp are hunger's teeth that man and wife / Draw lots who first shall die to lengthen life" until rescued by corn from Tyre, delivered by Pericles. One would think that that would ensure the eternal gratitude of Cleon, the ruler of Tharsus: it would seem a good place to stay were it not for the news that Antiochus' hired killer knows where he is – hence the moving on and the shipwreck which lands Pericles in Pentapolis, where nothing much seems wrong: Pericles wins the hand of Simonides' daughter, Thaisa, and Simonides, the king, is given the accolade "good... for his peaceable reign and good government" by one of his subjects, a lowly fisherman.

Unfortunately Pericles cannot stay at Pentapolis as he hears of unease at home in Tyre: maybe the absent prince should be permanently replaced by Helicanus, the Pericles-appointed substitute ruler: "kingdoms without a head, / Like goodly buildings left without a roof / Soon fall to ruin" is the argument relayed to Pericles by the loyal Helicanus, who had negotiated a breathing space of twelve months within which Pericles is to return home. It is on this return voyage that he loses Thaisa and lands at Tharsus again, fearing that

Marina will not survive the longer sea-journey to Tyre.

And eventually, sixteen years later, Tharsus too shows its ugly side. All Marina's excellences create envy in Creon and we see another manifestation of father/daughter love: not incest, not the idealism of Pericles and Marina, but this time what is a more everyday impulse of a father wanting to do the best for his daughter, wishing her to receive the respect and admiration due to her. Fair enough. But such is the "general wonder" felt for her companion Marina that Philoten is scarcely noticed. To rectify this Creon gives orders for the murder of Marina. Whatever the motive, there is manifestly no justification for the extreme reaction of Creon and his wife Dionyza.

So we have Creon and Dionyza (and Antiochus and his Daughter) representing flawed humanity, and we also have Antioch and Tharsus being seen as exhibiting corruption at the highest level of government. We have Pentapolis as an exemplar of good government; with regard to Mytilene I have my doubts about the governor, and Tyre seems to be governed pretty sensibly and pragmatically. A cross-section of a real world, contrasting with the idealism of the Pericles/Marina and Pericles/Thaisa world.

There is a disturbing real world too in the brothel in Mytilene. Marina's maidenhead is auctioned; she is advertised in the market: "He that will give most shall have her first!" The Bawd will give her instructions in how to please and "taste gentlemen of all fashions". Leaving Marina, invoking the aid of Diana, in this perilous situation, Shakespeare takes us for two scenes to Tharsus, where Creon and Dionyza show Pericles the inscribed tomb of Marina and he swears "Never to wash his face, nor cut his hairs", and to wear sackcloth. There is no doubt of the relevance of these scenes in Tarsus but while they are being enacted at least half the mind of the audience is in Mytilene, concerned about the fate of Marina. She was left in real danger, and although there is a good deal of humour in the brothel scenes it is a very edgy humour which does not disguise the threat to Marina's virginity. The humour affords the opportunity to release the audience's tension and fear, but the tension and fear are never far away. It is brilliant stagecraft and, like so much of *Pericles*, it is a very real world.

I have mentioned Marina's invoking Diana, the goddess of chastity, at a crucial moment in *Pericles*, and it is Diana who appears to Pericles in a vision in Act 5, exhorting him to visit her temple in Ephesus (where Thaisa is to be found). Neptune is also mentioned, not surprisingly, in context with "the sea-tossed Pericles". But probably the strongest influence on the happenings in *Pericles* is Fortuna or Lady Fortune. In his introductory Chorus to Act 3 Gower tells us that "Fortune's mood varies again" and, albeit unspecifically, Pericles accepts his fate when he says, "We cannot but obey the powers above us." Clearly Diana and Neptune play their part in *Pericles* – especially, I would argue, Diana. But that last quotation from the lips of Pericles is, I believe, the key to the play: accepting your Fortune or fate – as it is, ultimately, with Hamlet.

I have argued earlier about the impossibility of finding fault with Marina, Thaisa and Pericles: nothing they have done, nor anything in their characters, justifies the fates that befall them. Yet from all of them comes a fatalistic, stoic acceptance of their lot. No railing against the gods and injustice, not an ounce of self-pity. There is a moment when Pericles hears of the (apparent) death of Thaisa and calls out: " O you gods! / Why do you make us love your goodly gifts, / And snatch them straight away?" but immediately he responds to Lychorida's[20] invocation of patience and can be seen as a kind of male Griselda[21]. No more complaints, and for this, it would seem, his patience is rewarded. There is a good deal of discussion as to whether *Pericles* is a fable, a morality play or indeed a fairy story. In this context I think labels are odious. It is certainly a morality play in the sense that love conquers death and that patient suffering is rewarded. Perhaps a fable too as the journeys of Pericles can be seen as the life events of Everyman – it is our universal destiny to be beset by life and it is possible to survive the travails and come through it all with joy. I know fairy stories can be grim, but their grimness tends to be in a make-believe world, and so for me the realities, of incest and envy and putative murder disqualify *Pericles* being thought of as a fairy tale.

---

20   Marina's nurse.
21   Griselda is in folklore associated with long-suffering patience and obedience, and is probably best known from Chaucer's *The Clerk's Tale*.

Putting labels aside, it is the reward of suffering with joy that is absolutely central to *Pericles*, and it is a joy so great that it is heavenly and unquantifiable. This is why I think we should all see *Pericles*. There are other moving musical references in Shakespeare's plays: I am thinking especially of Caliban's talking of the music to be found on Prospero's island[22]; of Lorenzo's talking to Jessica in Act 5 Scene 1 of *The Merchant of Venice*. But it is in *Pericles* that all of us, along with Pericles, hear the music of the spheres at the exquisite and spiritually ravishing moment when Pericles and Marina are reunited. It is the "most heavenly music". Lear might die from joy in the belief that Cordelia lives, but Pericles is brought back to life in the knowledge that Marina is alive – and his joy can only be experienced by the exquisite harmony of the planets as they move in their ordered orbits, a music which few ever hear, but which Pericles certainly does in a truly heart-stopping moment. There are other aspects of *Pericles*, which I hope I have presented clearly, which justify a visit to a performance of the play, but none more so than the surge of spiritual joy which suffuses the end of the play.

Footnote:
There is much discussion about how much of *Pericles* was written by Shakespeare. What matters for me is that even if he lifted a good deal almost directly from other sources, it was a (popular contemporary) theme he wished to explore and at the very least he almost certainly wrote the last two acts.

---

22   So effectively used by Danny Boyle in the 2012 London Olympics opening ceremony.

Memorable Quotations From *Pericles*

Think death no hazard in this enterprise.
(Pericles)

For death remembered should be like a mirror,
Who tells us life's but breath, to trust it error.
(Pericles)

Few love to hear the sins they love to act.
(Pericles)

For vice repeated is like the wand'ring wind
Blows dust in others' eyes to spread itself.
(Pericles)

They do abuse the King that flatter him,
For flattery is the bellows blows up sin…
Whereas reproof, obedient and in order,
Fits kings, as they are men, for they may err.
(Helicanus)

'Tis time to fear when tyrants seems to kiss.
(Pericles)

…tyrants' fears
Decrease not, but grower faster than the years.
(Pericles)

For if a king bid a man be a villain, he's bound by the indenture of his oath
to be one.
(Thaliard)

...shall we rest us here,
And by relating tales of others' griefs,
See if 'twill teach us to forget our own?
(Cleon)

One sorrow never comes but brings an heir
That may succeed as his inheritor.
(Cleon)

Who makes the fairest show means most deceit.
(Cleon)

He is a happy king since he gains from his subjects the name of good by his
government.
(Pericles)

Opinion's but a fool that makes us scan
The outward habit for the inward man.
(Simonides)

...kingdoms without a head,
Like goodly buildings left without a roof
Soon fall to ruin.
(Second Lord)

O you gods!
Why do you make us love your goodly gifts,
And snatch them straight away?
(Pericles)

We cannot but obey the powers above us.
(Pericles)

Had I brought here a corrupted mind,
Thy speech had altered it.
(Lysimachus)

What would you have me do? Go to the wars, would you? Where a man
may serve seven years for the loss of a leg, and have not money enough in
the end to buy him a wooden one?

(Boult)

Prithee, speak.
Falseness cannot come from thee; for thou lookest
Modest as Justice, and thou seemest a palace
For the crowned Truth to dwell in.
(Pericles)

Give me a gash, put me to present pain;
Lest this great sea of joys rushing upon me
O'erbear the shores of my mortality,
And drown me with their sweetness.
(Pericles)

The music of the spheres!… I hear most heavenly music.
(Pericles)

Did you not name a tempest,
A birth and death?
(Thaisa)

You gods, your present kindness
Makes my past miseries sports.
(Pericles)

MEASURE FOR MEASURE

The initial premise behind these essays was that politicians can learn so much from Shakespeare's plays. Mainly what concerns me is their lack of exposure to a wide range of human beings and human emotions – the very stuff of literature – and the consequent alienation from most of the people on whom their policies will have an impact. But what is also true is that in addition to a profound understanding of people Shakespeare has much to contribute to any discussion of political problems and theories of government. And no play is more obviously concerned with these issues than *Measure for Measure*. How do you breathe new life into laws that have been allowed to drift into disuse? Is it better to pursue mercy or uncompromising justice? Is it healthy and appropriate for rulers to spy on their people in disguise? Should the law make any allowances for human frailty? Such are the very real concerns raised by this play, concerns that I hope are constantly in the minds of our lawmakers.

There are other questions raised too; chiefly concerned with sex. Is it wrong to have premarital sex? Are brothels acceptable outlets for the male libido? Is a sister's virginity to be prized more than a brother's life? This latter question is the axis around which the human drama of *Measure for Measure* spins.

The story of *Measure for Measure* is that of the Duke (of Venice) who has for fourteen years laxly neglected the enforcement of the law. So, on the pretext of a visit to Poland he deputes Angelo to rigorously enforce the laws that have fallen into abeyance, while he lurks in the shadows observing, and thus is privy to most of what is going on in Venice in his apparent absence. What goes on is the closing down of the brothels and the imprisonment and sentence to death of Claudio for impregnating his fiancée. On the advice of her brother's friend Lucio, Isabella – Claudio's sister and a novice nun – pleads to Angelo on her brother's behalf, to which Angelo's response is to lust after Isabella, and suggest that if she sleeps with him he will free her brother. Outraged, Isabella will have none of this. It is then contrived that Angelo sleeps with Mariana, to whom he had been contracted before her loss of dowry and who still loves him, believing her to be Isabella. Having, as he believes, slept with Isabella, Angelo then reneges on his promise to free Claudio and gives orders for his death, but is thwarted by an already dead pirate being presented as the decapitated Claudio. Fortunately the Duke has observed most of this, and so he 'returns' and Angelo is exposed, but in a round of happy endings Angelo is to marry Mariana, Claudio will marry his fiancée Juliet, Lucio will marry a prostitute and, it seems, the Duke will marry Isabella. (I will write more about these last two liaisons, but that, in essence is the story of the play.)

Some ten years earlier Shakespeare had juxtaposed the demands of justice and the letter of the law with pleas for mercy in *The Merchant of Venice*, and in *Measure for Measure* he returns to the theme. Angelo is simply enacting the letter of the law to have Claudio arrested and sentenced to death; in many ways this is the crackdown for which he was appointed but it does seem an excessive punishment, and indeed would have seemed so at the time, for common law practice was that sex before marriage simply established the certainty of the subsequent marriage. Escalus, appointed Angelo's second in command, has a much more moderate response to Claudio's crime, but Angelo turns to him, and somewhat smugly, boasts: "'Tis one thing to be tempted, Escalus, / Another thing to fall." Shortly after he meets Isabella, who causes his heart to beat faster, his loins to get excited and him to fall!

It is this imperfection in mankind that Shakespeare is constantly writing about. You cannot make and enforce laws based on human perfection. And Angelo is far from perfect. I have mentioned already how he is prepared to adjust the draconic laws he is imposing in order to satisfy his lust. Having, as he believes, ravished Isabella, he then reneges on his deal with her and does not rescind the death sentence on Claudio, being confident that his word rather than that of Isabella will be believed. It also comes to light that he had previously backed out of a marriage contract with Mariana once her dowry had been lost. He may be better versed than anyone in the common law but on a human level, this man does not seem to be worthy of being the Duke's substitute, albeit the Duke talks of having "lent him our terror". Terror is not the same as justice is not the same as mercy. Angelo, of whom Lucio says, "it is certain that when he makes water, his urine is congealed ice", is deservedly riding for a fall. It simply will not do to say that he is no more libidinous than Venice's other citizens: as a judge he should at least be nearly beyond reproach – though, as we have seen, Lear had some wise words on that subject.

It is true, though, that the society in which Angelo is living would appear to be especially libidinous. I am not referring to the premarital romp of Claudio and Juliet, but to the prevalence of Mistress Overdone and her brothel trade in *Measure for Measure*. Lucio claims to have purchased a multiplicity of diseases under Mistress Overdone's roof, and, although Angelo has given the order for all such "houses in the suburbs of Vienna [to be] plucked down", it seems that the brothels have become "hot houses" or bath houses (perhaps we would say massage parlours) and they are simply being relocated. Early in the play Mistress Overdone complains that "what with the war, what with the sweat, what with the gallows, and what with poverty, I am custom-shrunk", but her servant, Pompey, is content to ply his trade for he knows that testosterone-fuelled men will always need a sexual outlet and therefore brothels will always be viable: he jokes to Escalus vis-à-vis the shutting down of brothels - "Does your worship mean to geld and splay all the youth of the city?"

In fact at the time of the writing of *Measure for Measure* Mistress Overdone's complaints about her lack of trade were most relevant. I am talking of the winter 1603–1604. A war with Spain was coming to an end; trials for treason and potential executions for Raleigh and others were taking place in Winchester; and, most importantly, there was the spread of the plague, which led to many fleeing from London. Indeed by a proclamation of 16th September 1603 certain houses in the suburbs were to be pulled down to attempt to stop the spread of the plague by "dissolute and idle persons". So for Shakespeare's audience *Measure for Measure* was full of relevant, contemporary issues.

The spread of the plague is certainly not relevant today, but the licensing of brothels, whether to keep prostitutes off the streets and the issues of health and venereal disease, are all serious matters I would expect politicians to have views on. It is not an easy issue, but *Measure for Measure* certainly contributes to the debate.

What Angelo in his relentless pursuit of justice fails to take into account is the relativity of criminal acts, something which will always pose problems when a zero-tolerance policy is enacted. Taking a life by murder, for example, is significantly more vile than a premarital impregnation which creates rather than destroys life. I think there is little doubt where the sympathies of the majority[23] of Shakespeare's audience would have lain – producing progeny would have been seen as probably man's most important function. No children means no continuity of life. Whatever the Duke has to say, in his splendid philosophical speech about death, the continuation of the species – the significance of which, at times of the plague, is ratcheted up – has a paramountcy. The whole Death vs. Life theme is bubbling within the text of the play. (Isabella's prioritizing her own chastity over her brother's life of course contributes to this.) And what is certain is that Angelo's cold attitude towards life would not have received a sympathetic response from the audience at the Globe.

The response to Lucio, though, would have been much more mixed: indeed Shakespeare plays with the audience in his presentation of him and how he keeps defying our expectations. We meet him initially jesting with fellow brothel visitors, then we see him acknowledged by Claudio as a "good friend" who exhorts Isabella to "make friends to the strict deputy" and plead on her brother's behalf. He is present and acts as an encouraging commentator during Isabella's first interview with the Duke. Then, although Mistress Overdone's servant Pompey hails him as a friend, Lucio refuses to stand bail for him after his arrest as a whoremaster. There is a mocking jest in everything Lucio says and it culminates in his talking to the Duke-disguised-as-a-friar, failing to recognise the Duke, and gossiping totally false calumnies about the Duke – for example that he "would eat mutton on Fridays", i.e. visit prostitutes, although "he's now past

23   Although there was also a minority of strong-thinking puritans who would not have attended the theatre and saw the theatre as a place of sin, and the plague of the time as a consequence of this sin.

it". And once the Duke reveals himself, Lucio is sentenced to marry a punk (prostitute) for the offence of slandering a prince – perhaps an excessively cruel, and not entirely warranted, fate…

A man of many facets, albeit each one is coloured with humour. That is one of Lucio's – very important – functions in *Measure for Measure*; he is described in the Dramatis Personae as a Fantastic – that is, a fop; a vain young dandy. Yet even when he is digging himself a deeper hole by unknowingly slandering the Duke to his face, he talks some sense, as in "A little more lenity to lechery would do no harm" and "what a ruthless thing is this in him, for the rebellion of a codpiece to take away the life of a man". And he is fundamentally instrumental in the enactment of the drama, as he acts as a go-between for Claudio and Isabella, takes her to Angelo and there encourages her to pursue her suit. Even more than this it is he whose persistence ensures Claudio's survival. As Donald A. Stauffer[24] commented: "If it were not for this unprincipled rake, the two idealists would have killed Claudio between them." It is true that Shakespeare employs Lucio as a plot-agent and that once that role is over a kind of unpleasantness is seen in his dealings with Pompey, Mistress Overdone and the Duke. But there is always wit around Lucio and, at times, good sense. His character leaps out from the page or stage. I think he is the most interesting character in *Measure for Measure*.

That latter is plainly just a personal view. Isabella and the Duke are clearly rivals for that position too. I find it difficult to warm to Isabella, and I don't think this is simply 17th century morality being judged from the perspective of the 21st century. Let me explain. She is on the verge of becoming a novitiate nun and almost her first words are that she wishes there were "a more strict restraint upon the sisters". These are the words of an adolescent, fearing she needs more rules and discipline to keep potentially uncontrollable emotions under check. When pressed by Lucio to intervene with Angelo on her brother's behalf she rather weakly and unconfidently promises, "I'll see what I can do", and Lucio has to prompt her constantly in this initial interview with Angelo just to keep her going. It is true that Isabella does grow in confidence, but she is so unsure of herself. At one stage, in her second interview, she tells Angelo "I had rather

---

24   *Shakespeare's World of Images* (1949).

give my body than my soul", but when faced with the proposition that she does give her body in reality, that is when she iterates the heart-stopping "More than our brother is our chastity." Perhaps she was right first time about the preference of giving her body not her soul, and certainly that was contemporary thinking where chastity was seen as a state of mind rather than a state of body. It seems Isabella permitted a horror of having sex to be unworthily elevated to a principle which would have condemned her brother to death.

All this is very young, very adolescent. When told by Lucio of her brother's having gotten someone with child, she immediately knows that it must have been her cousin Juliet and her response is "O, let him marry her!" – the automatic reply of a young, worldly woman of the time, which is essentially what she is. Entering a nunnery would seem to be a not-very-clearly-thought-out adolescent response. She is aspiring to obtain spirituality without having first gained self-knowledge. What I am saying is that I don't think it is her role as a nun that presents her with the moral dilemma vis-à-vis her brother, I believe it is her sexual adolescence which presents the problem. She is very young. Whether that makes it more appropriate for the Duke to propose marriage to her – a very young woman as opposed to a would-be nun – is a moot point!

What of the Duke, then? Both in the context of a discussion of appropriate government, and of what was the recent accession of James I to the English throne, he is a fascinating character. He has been lax in enforcing certain laws and needs a more credible and firmer hand than his to start reinforcing these laws. Fair enough, but then he appoints Angelo – true, he could not anticipate his lusting after Isabella, but his behaviour with regard to Mariana should probably have cast doubts about his probity. The little we hear of Escalus' opinions inclines me to think he would have been a better choice as deputy. Be that as it may: the Duke appeared to want draconian, and he got draconian in spades.

Is it appropriate, then, for the Duke to disguise himself as a friar and to snoop on his people? We know the Duke sees himself as "a scholar, a statesman, and a soldier", but he also has a reputation of being "the old fantastical duke of dark corners". So hiding and disguising, observing, was his mode of seeing what was really

61

going on in Vienna. Is this a better way of gaining an understanding of the reality of society than, say, focus groups or Ken Livingstone travelling openly on the tube? How does a politician really gauge what the mood of the country is? I know film stars go out into the streets in disguise, but I am not aware of any politicians so doing. Anyway, in this case, in Vienna, it works – for the Duke gains a unique understanding of the machinations of Angelo.

In *Henry V*, before the battle of Agincourt, Shakespeare has the king in disguise – "a little touch of Harry in the night" – sounding out the morale of his troops. And the new king, James I, tried to visit the Exchange unobserved to view the activity of the merchants. Indeed *Measure for Measure* contains many similarities between the Duke of Vienna and James I. James I was a scholar, described as "a Living Library and a walking Study".[25] He was highly sensitive to slander (Jonson and Chapman's 1605 play *Eastward Ho* landed them in jail for unflattering comments about the Scots). When Raleigh and others were about to be executed for treason at Winchester James instituted a literally last-minute reprieve. Shakespeare and his company were appointed the King's Players at the outset of James I's reign; they enjoyed a privileged position, and, although the Duke is clearly not an exact portrait there are similarities both in character and in the morality of the times for Shakespeare to be slightly ingratiating himself with the king, *and* to be discussing relevant contemporary issues.

There are one or two other aspects of *Measure for Measure* which should be noted. As in *Othello* we have what is called a double-time scheme: for the watching audience it appears that the action is consecutively happening within a few days, whereas in reality the Duke was absent for much longer. Thematically we have an examination of the values of grace as a spiritual force and man's sex drive as a natural force. Virtue is seen as a mediator or moderator between these polarities: there is a middle way which does not permit spiritual zeal to become cold and selfish, nor will it permit the sex drive to descend into mere lechery. Yes, man possesses both spiritual and sexual drives, but both of these – see Isabella and Lucio – need to be integrated into a virtuous, outgoing self that functions

---

25 *The Summe and Substance of the Conference.... at Hampton Court: William Barlow* (1604).

maturely and responsibly in the world.

On a law-enforcement level too the middle way would seem to be the approved answer, by which I mean the direction towards which Shakespeare is pointing the audience – and James I? On one hand Angelo administers the letter of the law and will allow no extenuating circumstances, on the other Escalus is willing to excuse wrongdoers on the grounds that we all might succumb to temptation had we been in a certain place at a certain time. Real justice, for the individual and society, is to be found between these two extremes: wrongdoing should not be excused on the grounds of weak human nature, but nor should nature be ignored when sentencing.

Measure for Measure is about good government and an appropriate enacting of the laws. Those are the fundamental themes of the play – fitting themes for politicians. Politicians might baulk at the neat arranged marriages which conclude the play, none of which seems to me to begin to guarantee happiness, but most importantly what they – and all of us – can take from *Measure for Measure* is that politics must always take account of the individual and contemporary societal values. Angelo and Lucio, the Duke and Isabella might present the issues and all be fully realised characters, but it is the quality of the justice measured out to individuals such as Claudio and Juliet and Marina which determines the level of justice and civilisation in society.

Memorable Quotations From *Measure for Measure*

*There's not a soldier of us all that, in thanks giving before meat, do relish
the petition well that prays for peace.*
(1 Gent)

*Thus, what with the wars, what with the sweat, what with the gallows, and
what with poverty, I am custom-shrunk.*
(Mistress Overdone)

But what's his offence?
(Mistress Overdone)
Groping for trouts, in a peculiar river.
(Pompey)

Good counsellors lack no clients.
(Pompey)

*Whether that the body public be
A horse whereon the governor doth ride,
Who, newly in the seat, that it may know
He can command, lets it straight feel the spur.*
(Claudio)

Fewness and truth.
(Lucio)

*Lord Angelo: a man whose blood
Is very snow-broth; one who never feels
The wanton stings and motions of the sense...*
(Lucio)

We must not make a scarecrow of the law,
Setting it up to fear the birds of prey,
And let it keep one shape till custom make it
Their perch, and not their terror.
(Angelo)

'Tis one thing to be tempted, Escalus,
Another thing to fall.
(Angelo)

This will last out a night in Russia
When nights are longest there.
(Angelo)

Does your worship mean to geld and splay all the youth of the city?
(Pompey)

No ceremony that to great ones longs,
Not the king's crown, nor the deputed sword,
The marshal's truncheon, nor the judge's robe,
Become them with one half so good a grace
As mercy does.
(Isabella)

O, it is excellent
To have a giant's strength, but it is tyrannous
To use it like a giant.
(Isabella)

Thieves for their robbery have authority,
When judges steal themselves.
(Angelo)

More than our brother is our chastity.
(Isabella)

Be absolute for death…
…Merely, thou art Death's fool;
For him thou labour'st by thy flight to shun,
And yet run'st towards him still…
…Thy best of rest is sleep…
…If thou art rich, thou'rt poor;
For, like an ass whose back with ingots bows,
Thou bear'st thy heavy riches but a journey,
And Death unloads thee…
…Thou hast nor youth, nor age,
But as it were an after-dinner sleep,
Dreaming on both.
(Duke)

…it is certain that when he makes water, his urine is congealed ice.
(Lucio)

Though music oft hath such a charm
To make bad good, and good provoke to harm.
(Duke)

…you weigh equally: a feather will turn the scale.
(Provost)

…the old fantastical duke of dark corners.
(Lucio)

I am a kind of burr, I shall stick.
(Lucio)

…for truth is truth
To th'end of reck'ning.
(Isabella)

My lord, she may be a punk; for many of them are neither maid, widow nor wife.
(Lucio)

Cucullus non fachit monachum.
(Lucio)

Marrying a punk, my lord, is pressing to death,
Whipping, and hanging.
(Lucio)

Slandering a prince deserves it.
(Duke)

ANTONY AND CLEOPATRA

My love affair with *Antony and Cleopatra* – and specifically with the character of Cleopatra – began when I studied it for A Level with an inspiring teacher, Brian 'Harry' Holbeche, and was firmly cemented when I saw Helen Mirren playing the role in a National Youth Theatre production. My devotion has not since wavered. So there is a part of me wants to say to those who do not know the play "Just read/see *Antony and Cleopatra*; listen to the most memorable, uplifting, love-enhancing verse you will find anywhere. Open your heart, mind and soul to the splendour, magnificence and intensity of a love affair that is unrivalled in the political history of the world." Maybe the splendour of love is not a selling point for political leaders but I would hope the last four words of that last sentence would be enough of a hook to catch their interest. And, in truth, though I love the verse, the political content is fascinating and enlightening too.

This is a love affair between the most powerful of the Roman leaders and the enchanting Queen of Egypt, both of whom are ultimately prepared to risk the loss of power for the sake of their mutual love. And in the course of the play we see, again, a commentary on the fickle nature of the mob; we see how unsuccessful leaders can no longer command loyalty; we see how defectors can be used ruthlessly by the side to which they have defected; we see how acceptable dirty tricks can be, provided leaders appear to have no prior knowledge of it; we see leaders lying and deceiving in order to gain advantage; and we also see nobility and honour in action. Much indeed for politicians to think on.

The story is simple, alternating between the worlds of Rome and Egypt, the world of governmental pragmatism and the world of luxury and indulgence. At the start of the play Antony is revelling in Egypt with Cleopatra, while Caesar[26] (one part of the governing triumvirate with the ineffective Lepidus and Antony) is in Rome attempting to deal with the rebellious Pompey. Then Antony hears news of the death of his abandoned wife Fulvia and returns dutifully to Rome. In Rome he makes peace with an angry Caesar and cements his relationship with Caesar by marrying his sister Octavia. Peace with Pompey is made aboard his yacht, but then the lure of the East calls Antony back to Cleopatra. Abandoning Caesar's sister is the final straw to break the Antony/Caesar relationship and their armies come to blows on land and, mainly, at sea. Antony's followers desert him, including the (almost) ever-faithful Enobarbus, and Antony botches his suicide attempt. Dying, he is carried to Cleopatra, whereon follows the most wonderful expressions of love. Cleopatra, on Antony's death, seems to be making some kind of a deal with Caesar, but prepares to meet Antony in death and kills herself with an asp to her breast.

That's it. I find almost every line in *Antony and Cleopatra* memorable and I think I committed an act of cruelty to the text by cutting out so much memorable poetry in my list of quotations, for example all those dots in the last speech of Cleopatra I have quoted. Be that as it may, let us look at the political/thematic issues.

The first thing to note is how a love affair can ruin the life and reputation of any person in power. I am not talking about an obscure gay Welsh MP picking up a bit of rough on Wimbledon Common or indeed John Profumo and Christine Keeler: these are minor figures and indiscretions when compared to the relationship between Antony and Cleopatra. So, again by comparison, was the relationship between Charles Stewart Parnell and Kitty O'Shea, which effectively destroyed Parnell's power. All these were illicit and secret relationships – as indeed was that between John Major and Edwina Currie which, curiously, might well have enhanced each's pygmy reputation. Antony and Cleopatra made no secret of their relationship. Enobarbus tells us of the magnificent public display which was Cleopatra in her barge on the River Cydnus, travelling to meet Antony for the first time. We know that together

---

26   I have used the name Caesar: he is Julius Caesar's nephew and has the full name Octavius Caesar and is also known as Octavius.

they entertain kings and reel the streets at noon. It may seem to cerebral observers that this triumvir – "triple pillar of the world" – has been transformed into "a strumpet's fool". But to the two of them, as they carouse and cross-dress together, their love appears rooted in and blessed by heaven. No holding back their passion; no secret love in dark, hidden corners. Their joy is manifest and manifested for the world to see, and they had unequalled power in Rome and the East. They are the archetypes of those who lose themselves in love and, in so doing, lose all. Through them we can see how disastrous our own mixing of politics and extramarital love might be. But it is possible we might think the world well lost if we had experienced the overwhelming love that these two most famous lovers shared…

It is long odds-on, though, that almost all of us cannot even aspire to that state of ecstasy; so for us dull sublunary lovers the love between Antony and Cleopatra is a potent warning of the consequences of entangling work with extramarital delights. There is also a warning about each of us staying within the sphere we naturally inhabit. Antony is the military man – that is his sphere of expertise – yet Cleopatra decides to join him with her fleet in the sea battle of Actium against Caesar. And at a crucial, evenly balanced time in the battle, she turns tail in fear and Antony – "my heart was to thy rudder tied by th'strings" – follows her, with the result that not only is his generalship besmirched, so is his honour. Moral? Keep business and pleasure well apart and don't interfere in a partner's area of expertise.

Is there anything to learn from these two about folly and age? There is no hint of senility or mental frailty as there was with Lear, but Cleopatra looks back on her "salad days when I was green in judgment" and Antony contrasts his "grizzled head" with the "boy Caesar… wear[ing] the rose of youth upon him". In fact most estimates have Cleopatra at thirty-eight years of age and Antony at forty-three. Yes, it is a middle-aged love affair. We remember – and forgive ourselves – the times when we were young and foolish, doing extravagant things for love and counting neither the cost nor the consequences. We forgive our children too and indeed all young people who are encountering certain feelings and their strength for the first time. But by the time middle age has arrived, perhaps we are muttering that would-be lovers should by now have got some kind of hold on their feelings and be able to control them and behave with a certain dignity. Perhaps... I personally rejoice in the sublimity – and the reality – of Antony and Cleopatra's love affair: I don't care a jot how old the two protagonists are. But if you are a grey-suited career politician I guess you should take heed and keep your sexual passions within approved limits!

But love, as an energising force, is useless in battle – indeed in this instance it energises retreat and apparent cowardice. How far has macho bravery plummeted from the days when Antony – according to Caesar – drank horse's urine and ate "strange flesh, which some did die to look on". Antony knows that he has sacrificed his honour at the altar of love – we are told that the strange music we hear is an indication of the god Hercules leaving him. Yet he has not lost his greatness, demonstrated by his magnanimity when the faithful Enobarbus finally leaves Antony and Antony sends greetings and his treasure after him, acknowledging that his "fortunes have corrupted honest men".

Once followers know that their leader's fortunes are on the wane, there can be a rush to be dissociated from the leader – witness the falling away from Margaret Thatcher in 1990 and three cabinet resignations within a week as Gordon Brown's ill-fated premiership struggled on. In *Antony and Cleopatra* not only is the foolishness of following a fading leader demonstrated by the defection of Enobarbus but we also see Seleucus, Cleopatra's treasurer, refusing to back up her stories to Caesar about the extent of her fortune. Fair enough, you might say: it's always important to know on which side your bread is buttered or in which direction the wind is blowing, or some similar time-serving acceptance of a new reality. Caesar would agree: indeed he expressly approves of Cleopatra trying to keep back for herself some of her own treasure. This, though, is the same Caesar who intends to renege on the promises he has made to Cleopatra and who previously had put all the defectors from Antony's army in Caesar's own front lines so "that Antony may seem to spend his fury upon himself". A cold, calculating Caesar – he is reluctant to wash his brain with wine during the festivities on board Pompey's yacht – and a pragmatist to the core, in total contrast to Mark Antony. No Machiavellian calculating[27] for him. In contrast, ruled by his passions, Antony possesses an admirable energy, generosity and magnanimity.

(Of course, being ruled by your passions means that mistakes are made: I have mentioned his faulty generalship in the Battle of Actium. There is also his dying advice to Cleopatra: "None about Caesar trust but Proculeus" – in fact Proculeus does Caesar's bidding exactly and it is Dolabella who helps Cleopatra's understanding of Caesar's double-dealing and his intentions for her, which is to lead her in triumph through all his conquered territories and finally put her on display in Rome.)

Do politicians believe opinion polls? They may well affect a casualness towards them, but I suspect they take note. We have seen in *Coriolanus* how easily swayed the mob may be and both Antony and Caesar express at different times how the "slippery people" are inclined to withhold their support until the object of their support has become a loser, and how they rock backwards and forwards indeterminately upon contemporary tides. What sways the masses? A question that any politician would give his hind teeth for the answer to. Focus groups are an attempt to find the answer, but there is manifestly no exact science to be applied. What *Antony and Cleopatra* does is yet again to raise the issues of popularity and the fickleness of political and popular support.

It also raises the issue of dirty tricks and how leaders can get away with treachery. I have already mentioned Caesar's deviousness: how he placed those who defected from Antony in his own front line and how he lied to Cleopatra about his intentions for her. What I think is even more significant in the "Who the hell can you trust?" world of politics is the scene aboard Pompey's yacht when a peace deal is being struck between Pompey and the triumvirate: savouring Pompey's hospitality are the "three world sharers" of the Roman world, in Pompey's hands. A sober Menas suggests to his somewhat drunken master Pompey that if he, Menas, cuts the cable and the yacht drifts out to sea then they can cut the throats of the

27   The question of Antony's marriage to Octavia is contentious. He makes it for immediate political convenience, but is it calculated in a Machiavellian way? Perhaps he is just not thinking ahead…

triumvirs and the world is Pompey's. Pompey's response is that it is a splendid idea and he wishes Menas had done it without telling him, for it would have been perceived as villainy had Pompey done it, but simply service had Menas unilaterally done it. The point being that the vilest of deeds is acceptable provided that it cannot be traced back to the leader – the leader must keep his own hands clean.

Well! If this is the way the scheming politician thinks it puts a dent in theories about idealism in politics. Can it be true that staying in power is the number one concern of politicians and that doing so depends largely on keeping up appearances? Is our current Prime Minister more concerned about the possible fallout from his associations with Rebekah Brooks, the Murdoch Empire and Andy Coulson than with solving the recession? Will Jeremy Hunt take enough of the flack from the BSkyB affair to leave Cameron untouched? I throw in these questions simply to illustrate that the deviousness of politicians and their getting someone else to do their (untraceable) dirty work has been current for centuries. It is not surprising in a post Stalin, Hitler and Mao world – and a world in which George W. Bush condones torture as a means of obtaining information. There are so many examples of how power corrupts and throws moral values to dogs as bones, and yet there are examples of idealism in politics which run counter to the double-dealing of political leaders on which I have been focusing. I will leave the reader to supply her/his own and make Mark Antony my only suggestion, though there has to be a question mark over his marriage to Octavia. Political double-dealing, nonetheless, is a major issue in *Antony and Cleopatra*.

This play also raises the question of when it is best to retire, or perhaps to accept that your glory days are over. Antony's past military triumphs – at Pharsalia and Philippi for example – are forgotten and he is remembered as the lover of Cleopatra, which led him to lose all his military acumen and to forfeit his reputation. Should he not have forsworn his responsibilities vis-à-vis governing the Eastern part of the Roman Empire and retired to the softness of Cleopatra's bed? Maybe, had that happened, it is unlikely that Caesar would have left him in peace, but the issue of when to retire is nonetheless prevalent in *Antony and Cleopatra*. People in power tend to cling on to power and in so doing frequently lose any honourable reputation they once may have had – so many African despots are evidence to that.

But it could be argued that Antony's reputation is actually enhanced by his being linked with Cleopatra as two of the greatest ever lovers. John Dryden called his 1678 play about Antony and Cleopatra *All for Love or The World Well Lost*: the title itself epitomises one way of responding to their story. But these are two people well past their youthful prime; Antony's feelings are described as being "dotage" and Cleopatra is variously called a whore, a filthy nag, a right gypsy, half-blasted and a boggler (the latter three by Antony). Are we actually watching the folly of two older people whose lives and reputations are disintegrating before our eyes? Is any woman worth such a loss of reputation as is visited upon Antony? Is any man worth the uninhibited passion poured upon him as Cleopatra does with Antony? Surely – like the boy Caesar – we should be pouring scorn on their folly and dereliction of duty?

There is only one response to such an argument and that is the one word: Cleopatra. Respond to her in the play. I have been trying to persuade people to see/read *Antony and Cleopatra* for reasons of political and power relevance, and I hope such people have read thus far. For now I confess that the overwhelming reason for engaging with this play is to feel the glory and the passion of these magnificent people in love. Shakespeare's verse will blow your mind. Where soldiers meet, Cleopatra is the subject of discussion. Having described her majestic appearance when she meets Mark Antony for the first time, Enobarbus continues:

Age cannot weary her, nor custom stale
Her infinite variety: other women cloy
The appetites they feed, but she makes hungry
Where most she satisfies.

You never tire of her: she never sates your appetite. She is described as "a wonderful piece of work". Of course when things go wrong she is rounded on and blamed and insulted – mainly on a sexual level – but that references her power and the excitement that surrounds her.

Cleopatra plays billiards; she cross-dresses; she can hop forty paces through the streets without losing her breath; she has drunk Antony to his bed. Of course Caesar and the world of Rome cannot appreciate this lifestyle. Caesar implores Antony to "leave his lascivious wassails" – his life of voluptuous excess, where he "fishes, drinks and wastes the lamps of night in revel". That is Egypt and the world of Cleopatra. As A. C. Bradley writes: "She lives for feeling."

Yes, Cleopatra will flirt and double-deal to try to get her own way, but this is after the loss of Antony. Before that she is completely his: she writes to him every day and asks for the drug mandragora to drink that she "may sleep out this great gap of time my Antony is away". After Antony's defeat she joins him in mocking the midnight bell with their "one other gaudy night" together, and when he dies her encomium could not be more loving and splendid: she likens him to the sun and moon that give light to the earth; she talks of his military might; his musical – and earth-shaking - voice; his generosity; the beyond human delights of shared pleasures.[28] And when she dies she dons her robe and crown, as it were to meet Antony again at Cydnus, but this time in death as she hears him calling. "Husband, I come," she proclaims.

Cleopatra is all woman. Forget the issues of age and probity – would not any man wish to be in a relationship with her? At times frustrating and infuriating, but completely energising. At times calculating and bullying (witness her treatment of the messenger who brings news of Antony's marriage to Octavia), but always alive and loving. This is a play about passion and poetry, and Shakespeare gives us both in these wonderful creations of Antony and Cleopatra. *Antony and Cleopatra* is fundamentally a play about two people, two rulers and lovers, set on a political stage. And of course, the personal is political.

---

28   The relevant speech is Act 5 Scene 2 l.79–92.

Memorable Quotations From *Antony and Cleopatra*

There's beggary in the love that can be reckoned.
(Antony)

He was disposed to mirth; but on the sudden
A Roman thought hath struck him.
(Cleopatra)

She is cunning past man's thought.
(Antony)

The tears live in an onion that should water this sorrow.
(Enobarbus)

This common body,
Like to a vagabond flag upon the stream,
Goes back and forth…
(Caesar)

I was a morsel for a monarch.
(Cleopatra)

My salad days
When I was green in judgment.
(Cleopatra)

That truth should be silent I had almost forgot.
(Enobarbus)

...we did sleep day out of countenance and made the night light with drinking.
(Enobarbus)

For her own person,
It beggared all description.
(Enobarbus)

Age cannot weary her, nor custom stale
Her infinite variety: other women cloy
The appetites they feed, but she makes hungry
Where most she satisfies.
(Enobarbus)

I have not kept my square, but that to come
Shall all be done by th'rule.
(Antony)

I' th' East my pleasure lies.
(Antony)

Give me some music: music, moody food
Of us that trade in love.
(Cleopatra)

The beds i' th' East are soft.
(Antony)

But there is never a fair woman has a true face.
(Enobarbus)

It's monstrous labour when I wash my brain
And it grows fouler.
(Caesar)

The April's in her eyes: it is love's spring.
(Antony)

If I lose mine honour,
I lose myself.
(Antony)

You come not like Caesar's sister.
(Caesar)

Celerity is never more admired
Than by the negligent.
(Cleopatra)

Trust not to rotten planks.
(Soldier)

We have kissed away
Kingdoms and provinces.
(Scarus)

Egypt, thou knew'st too well
My heart was to thy rudder tied by th' strings.
(Antony)

'Tis better playing with a lion's whelp
Than with an old one dying.
(Enobarbus)

You have been a boggler ever.
(Antony)

For I am sure,
Though you can guess what temperance should be,
You know not what it is.
(Antony)

Let's have one other gaudy night: call to me
All my sad captains; fill our bowls once more;
Let's mock the midnight bell.
(Antony)

O, my fortunes have corrupted honest men!
(Antony)

She, Eros, has packed cards with Caesar.
(Antony)

Unarm, Eros. The long day's task is done,
And we must sleep.
(Antony)

I am dying, Egypt, dying.
Give me some wine, and let me speak a little.
(Antony)

And there is nothing left remarkable
Beneath the visiting moon.
(Cleopatra)

What's brave, what's noble,
Let's do't after the high Roman fashion,
And make death proud to take us.
(Cleopatra)

You gods will give us some faults to make us men.
(Agrippa)

You lie, up to the hearing of the gods.
(Cleopatra)

He words me, girls, he words me.
(Cleopatra)

Finish, good lady, the bright day is done,
And we are for the dark.
(Iras)

...I have
Immortal longings in me... methinks I hear
Antony call... Husband I come...
I am fire, and air; my other elements I give to baser life.
(Cleopatra)

No grave upon the earth shall clip in it
A pair so famous.
(Caesar)

AS YOU LIKE IT

Titling the play *As You Like It* might very well appeal to politicians: the apparently throwaway title would seem to be pandering to the audience, giving them what they want, which is what politicians of all parties do – attempting to give the public what they are perceived as wanting and therefore likely to vote for – in order to get elected. *As You Like It,* though, was in fact not popular with audiences until the 18th century: it was probably first performed at the Globe Theatre (newly opened) in 1599 and then there is no irrefutable record of its having been subsequently performed for over a century. There was a vogue for pastoral and Robin Hood plays at the time of the writing of *As You Like It* and I guess that accounts for its being so titled – just a casual, throwaway title, but one that does in reality stay firmly in the mind.

Leaving aside the title of the play, the content might at first sight appear to have little relevance to a modern audience looking for something significant in its themes. The first Act of *As You Like It* takes place in a usurping Duke's court: he has banished his brother to the forest of Arden where (almost) the rest of the play is set. The Duke sees his own daughter, and only child, Celia outshone by Rosalind, Celia's bosom friend, and so banishes Rosalind. Celia decides to accompany Rosalind into the forest, taking with them a court jester, Touchstone. Parallel to this family disagreement is the filial hostility of Oliver de Boys towards his younger brother Orlando – hostility to the extent that he encourages the Duke's wrestler to kill Orlando in a wrestling match. Against all the odds Orlando wins, but his father was the Duke's enemy so Orlando too leaves the court, accompanied by a faithful old servant, Adam. But before then, Orlando and Rosalind's eyes have met lovingly, and their romance is developed in the forest. However there is a complication, which is that Rosalind, for safety, has disguised herself as a boy, and as well as there being commentaries on the nature of pastoral life, and a more cynical commentary from Jaques in his 'seven ages of man' speech, the rest of the play is basically a comedy about multiple fallings in love and mistaken identities, all moving to a happy (and matrimonial) resolution, with Orlando and Oliver also being reconciled and the usurped Duke regaining his position as the usurper is converted to a pastoral life.

All fun and friendly, with a happy ending? Maybe, but within *As You Like It* are themes which warrant serious consideration: there is the question of the abuse of power; envy; friendship as opposed to consanguinity; the values within rural/pastoral life; the power of love, yet stripping away sentimentality from love; loyalty; an opposition between a cheerful optimism and cynicism; and resolution through love, forgiveness and reconciliation. In addition to this there is much humour (most of which does not work for a contemporary audience) and more music in the form of songs (all of which *do* work) than in any other Shakespeare play. If I had to describe *As You Like It* in one word it would be 'delightful' – but let us begin to look at the serious issues raised.

The abuse of power. We witness this in the first place in the usurper Duke Frederick. We are not given any reasons for his exiling of his brother, other than such an exile was "unjust". But we witness his injustice in the way he banishes Rosalind for no better reason than he mistrusts her as she is her father's daughter and "the people praise her for her virtues, / And pity her for her good father's sake". These are the words of Le Beau, one of Frederick's courtiers, who also warns Orlando of the Duke's undeserved antipathy towards him and that it were best to leave the court. In connection too with Orlando we also witness injustice with regard to Oliver's treatment of his younger brother whose "father charged [Oliver] in his will to give [Orlando] good education", whereas in fact Orlando is left to feed with Oliver's hinds. The reasons Oliver gives Charles the wrestler to dispose of Orlando are that he is "a secret and villainous contriver against me", but he admits later that Orlando has such nobility about him and is so beloved that he, Oliver, by comparison fails to receive sufficient recognition. It is the same argument used by Duke Frederick to his daughter Celia: that Rosalind "robs thee of thy name". It is an argument, of course, found in *Pericles* too, when

Dionyza arranges for Marina to be murdered as, by comparison with Marina, her own daughter Philoten is underappreciated.

This injustice in *As You Like It* is perhaps best seen in Oliver's treatment of the old family servant Adam, after he has tried to suggest the brothers behave peaceably towards each other. Oliver rejects him; calls him an "old dog" as a reward for his service. Injustice abounds. Something is rotten in the court of Duke Frederick. What is salutary in all this is the reinforcement of a recurrent theme in Shakespeare's plays: those in positions of power sooner or later forget basic common decency and morality, and will perpetrate injustices. Loyalty will no longer be recognised as a virtue. Every politician should take note.

Love – its power and its silliness – pervades, as you would expect, the romance *As You Like It*. Rosalind is at the centre of it. Although it is Phebe who quotes Marlowe: "Who ever lov'd that lov'd not at first sight?", it is Rosalind's response to Orlando which epitomises this dictum and sets up the romantic involvements: Rosalind is disguised as a male youth, causing the shepherdess Phebe to fall for 'him'; Silvius is in love with Phebe, with little prospect of reward; Touchstone, for apparently selfish sexual reasons, claims affection for the goatherd Audrey; Celia and Oliver, at the end of the play, find an instant attraction to each other; and, of course, Orlando is hopelessly in love with Rosalind, without recognizing her in her male disguise. All these relationships are brought to a married conclusion. So, on the surface it might appear that, although there is much comedy in these (sometimes misplaced) attractions, Shakespeare is ultimately endorsing not only the power but also the validity of head-over-heels romantic love.

But Shakespeare is never as simple as that. Rosalind, besides being a lover, is also a teacher. She has to teach Phebe not to scorn and belittle Silvius' love for her; she has to check out the seriousness of Orlando's love: that his love is not that of an adolescent poseur self-indulgently writing pretty awful romantic verses. There is the realism of Touchstone too, both acknowledging that it is the likely lot of men to be cuckolded, and eager to be married by an incompetent country vicar for "it will be a good excuse for me hereafter to leave my wife". And, finally, there is Rosalind recognizing the universal madness of love, but then getting real: "Men have died from time to time and worms have eaten them, but not for love."

This is the many-faceted Shakespeare, coming at the reader/spectator with views from all angles, showing and accepting the multiplicity of responses to life's experiences and condemning none. There is, for example, a lovely relationship between Rosalind and her cousin Celia in which it would appear that Shakespeare is extolling friendship above father/daughter ties, and this questioning of the traditional duties in family relationships is seen too in the appalling treatment that Oliver metes out to his younger brother. Yet by the conclusion of *As You Like It* "kindness... and nature" have seen Orlando risk his own life by saving a sleeping Oliver from a predatory lion and the two brothers are reconciled. Shakespeare's world is not one of absolutes, where friendship is more highly esteemed than consanguinity and duty; it is a world where you have a number of manifestations of different relationships and in which conflicts can be reconciled.

There is a similar complexity when we look at the alternatives of court and country life in *As You Like It*. Initially it might seem that this is a pastoral idyll, with all the unpleasantness and corruption being found solely in the first Act at court, whereas as soon as we turn to the Forest of Arden we hear Duke Senior extolling the virtues of the country life:

> *Are not these woods*
> *More free from peril than the envious court?*
> *...And this our life, exempt from public haunt,*
> *Finds tongues in trees, books in the running brooks,*
> *Sermons in stones, and good in everything.*

But this is exactly where it is important not to jump to conclusions: we must hold our horses and pause... Because the Duke and his followers have had to go into compulsory exile and have had to make the best of their life in Arden, living in a cave, but once the prospect of returning to court is offered at the end of *As You Like It* there is not a scintilla of doubt as to which style of life is preferred. There is no difficult decision (should I stay or should I go?) to be made: life at court wins hands down.

I think there is too strong an emphasis placed on the court vs. country theme. Adam, after all, very nearly died in Arden and his loyalty to Orlando is a loyalty forged in the non-Arden world. Similarly Celia's loyalty to Rosalind, though it continues in Arden, is also forged in the world of the court. Having said that, there is the instance of Corin, an exemplar of the goodness and honesty that a simple country life can give: "Sir, I am a true labourer: I earn that I eat, get that I wear; owe no man hate, envy no man's happiness; glad of other men's good, content with my harm; and the greatest of my pride is to see my ewes graze and my lambs suck." But then Phebe and Silvius and Audrey[29] are also dwellers in Arden; all merely human and flawed people – such people who are found the world over, whether in the forest or in the court.

Which is very much the point: Shakespeare is again refusing to simplify and judge. We can probably say that the Duke and his followers and Oliver are better for their Arden experience, but what about Touchstone? His loyalty to Celia means he accompanies her into the forest of Arden, but once there he misuses his acquired courtliness to impress a gullible Audrey for copulative purposes. Touchstone is ambivalent about the shepherd's life: talking to Corin he says, "Now in respect it is in the fields, it pleaseth me well; but in respect it is not in the court, it is tedious." Perhaps Corin can be given the last word on the court/country opposition: "Those that are good manners at the court are as ridiculous in the country as the behaviour of the country is most mockable at the court." Different worlds, different standards, different values: neither world is necessarily superior. I think we should be careful not to overestimate the goodness of the country life – Shakespeare doesn't.

Touchstone is a good example of the complexity of Shakespeare's characterization. I have mentioned his loyalty to Celia in contrast to his eagerness to take advantage of Audrey. He is also at the centre of much of the verbal comedy of *As You Like It*, though in truth there is much to be said for George Bernard Shaw's comment on Touchstone's humour: "Who would endure such humour from

---

29   In my experience Audrey is usually played wrongly. The text tells us that she acknowledges her lack of beauty and prizes honesty. It is Touchstone who wishes her to become sluttish. Audrey is more concerned with doing things correctly and getting married. Her simplicity lends her to being used by Touchstone.

anyone but Shakespeare? – an Eskimo would demand his money back if a modern author offered him such fare." Time has passed since Shaw's dictum but time has not improved Touchstone's humour, and a director would be well advised to do some savage cutting thereof. Having said all that, Shakespeare also gives Touchstone some memorable human insights, such as "The fool doth think he is wise, but the wise-man knows himself to be a fool." One categorises Shakespeare at one's peril!

The songs – of which there are more in *As You Like It* than in any other Shakespeare play – all very much contribute to the ambivalences within the play. There is a very simple song of joy and good cheer at the end of *As You Like It* when two Pages sing of:

> *...spring-time, the only pretty ring-time,*
> *When birds do sing, hey ding a ding, ding,*
> *Sweet lovers love the spring.*

But the two songs from earlier in the play contribute a more sombre note. In the first song Amiens sings of how under the greenwood tree no enemies other than the weather are to be found, but Jaques intervenes and sings his own last stanza, suggesting that a man who leaves behind his "wealth and ease" will find under the greenwood tree many fools similar to himself. Most telling, I think, is the song *Blow, blow, thou winter wind*, where the really painful issues of life are raised; in this context Amiens is not singling out the weather but "man's ingratitude" and "friends remember'd not", and he adds the comment "Most friendship is feigning, most loving mere folly." It is our mistreatment of each other that causes most pain and hardship (something with which Lear in the storm on the blasted heath would totally concur), not the wind and the cold. Such distressing, inhuman behaviour happens everywhere and there is therefore an irony in the concluding couplet of each stanza: "Then heigh-ho the holly, / This life is most jolly."

The songs in *As You Like It* are delightful, but they are not escapist songs. There may be music in Arden, but the songs too contribute towards the discussion of the serious values that represent the high points and the low points of human life and behaviour. And just in case any reader is still (falsely) luxuriating in the escape to Arden and uncomplicated simplicity you think it represents, let me finally remind you that lions are to be found roving there!

Arden does, though, provide the location for learning and gaining understanding; the passing of time, of which the audience is scarcely aware, also contributes to this increasing wisdom. I have already mentioned how Rosalind educates Phebe and Orlando. In addition Orlando's kind and noble nature responds to fraternal promptings and he not only rescues but forgives his brother; the brother, Oliver, in turn both responds to the Duke's hospitality and exhortations to love his brother but also falls immediately in love with the dowerless Celia so that the two cannot be parted. And overall it would seem that Duke Senior has learned patience and endurance, accepting what nature and the elements have thrown at him.

For there is so much good-heartedness in *As You Like It*. The vitality of Rosalind dominates the play: she takes control of most of the action and organizes those around her, always with wit and good humour. The overriding feel one gets from *As You Like It* is one of warmth and ultimate acceptance. Yet, there is Jaques – and there is no doubt of the cynicism of his 'seven ages of man' speech: after the "slipper'd pantaloon" stage we have "the last scene of all… second childishness and mere oblivion, / Sans teeth, sans eyes, sans taste, sans everything".

Indeed, everywhere in the play Jaques, though once a sensual libertine, is a highly critical observer of everyone's follies: Orlando calls him "Monsieur Melancholy", and Jaques admits that he loves melancholy "better than laughing". So, can it be argued that the character of Jaques runs counter to the general good-humoured tone of the play? Not quite, for he too provides a certain (caustic) wit and a wry commentary. The note he contributes to the harmony of the play is somewhat discordant but it enhances the texture of the music, and he genuinely values the freedom and the learning to be gained from being in Arden – so much so that he opts not to return to court but to stay in the forest with the newly arrived Duke Frederick: "…out of these convertites, / There is so much to be heard and learn'd".

Jaques is "for other than dancing measures" at the end of *As You Like*

It, but he is no Mercutio invoking "a plague o' both your houses" as he dies, nor is he the humiliated and angry Malvolio stomping off stage declaiming "I'll be revenged on the whole pack of you." Jaques just returns to the Duke's cave and will continue his life of learning and wry amusement at human folly.

No, *As You Like It* is such a good-natured play. With the exception of Jaques[30] all those whose behaviour we have witnessed in the forest are united in a final dance, and most of them in marriage. The worst offenders of the court in the first Act – Duke Frederick and Oliver – have been transformed, and the daftness of much of the behaviour in Arden may have been gently satirised, but all the characters have been accepted and forgiven. Indeed there is an all round forgiveness and reconciliation. Apart from a justifiable dig at Touchstone, Jaques concludes by wishing everyone well; so should we. Shakespeare frequently concludes his plays with a coming together and resolution, but whereas in plays such as *King Lear* and *Hamlet* there are enormous question marks hanging over what might happen next, in *As You Like It* there are no such qualms. It is after all a romantic comedy – and a brilliant, life-enhancing one at that!

---

30   Adam is not there either – his absence is best explained by the likelihood that the same actor played Adam and Jaques de Boys (who makes a brief expository appearance at the end).

Memorable Quotations From *As You Like It*

*...the good hussif Fortune... those she makes fair, she scarce makes honest;
and those she makes honest, she makes very ill-favouredly.*
(Celia)

Thus must I from the smoke into the smother...
(Orlando)

Treason is not inherited, my lord...
(Rosalind)

*And this our life, exempt from public haunt,
Finds tongues in trees, books in the running brooks,
Sermons in stones, and good in everything.*
(Duke Senior)

Beauty provokes thieves sooner than gold.
(Rosalind)

*O good old man, how well in thee appears
The constant service of the antique world,
When service sweat for duty, not for meed,
Thou art not for the fashion of these times,
Where none will sweat but for promotion.*
(Orlando)

We that are true lovers run into strange capers.
(Touchstone)

*And so from hour to hour, we ripe, and ripe,
And then from hour to hour, we rot, and rot,
And thereby hangs a tale.*
(Jaques)

...we are not all alone unhappy:
This wide and universal theatre
Presents more woeful pageants than the scene
Wherein we play in.
(Duke Senior)

All the world's a stage,
And all the men and women merely players.
They have their exits and their entrances...
(Jaques)

Blow, blow, thou winter wind,
Thou art not so unkind
As man's ingratitude...
Heigh-ho, sing heigh-ho, unto the green holly
Most friendship is feigning, most loving mere folly...
Freeze, freeze, thou bitter sky,
That does not bite so nigh
As benefits forgot...
Thy sting is not so sharp
As friends remember'd not.
(Jaques)

Those that are good manners at the court are as ridiculous in the country
as the behaviour of the country is most mockable at the court.
(Corin)

It is as easy to count atomies as to resolve the propositions of a lover.
(Celia)

Love is merely a madness, and... deserves as well a dark house and a whip
as madmen do.
(Rosalind)

I am not a slut, though I thank the gods I am foul.
(Audrey)
Well, praised be the gods for thy foulness; sluttishness may come
hereafter.
(Touchstone)

Sell when you can, you are not for all markets.
(Rosalind)

I am falser than vows made in wine.
(Rosalind)

Who ever lov'd that lov'd not at first sight?
(Phebe, quoting Marlowe's *Hero and Leander*)

I had rather have a fool to make me merry than experience to make me sad, and to travel for it too!
(Rosalind)

Men have died from time to time and worms have eaten them, but not for love.
(Rosalind)

Can one desire too much of a good thing?
(Rosalind)

Men are April when they woo, December when they wed. Maids are May when they are maids, but the sky changes when they are wives.
(Rosalind)

Many will swoon when they do look on blood.
(Oliver)

The fool doth think he is wise, but the wise-man knows himself to be a fool.
(Touchstone)

But O, how bitter a thing it is to look into happiness through another man's eyes!
(Orlando)

In spring-time, the only pretty ring-time,
When birds do sing, hey ding a ding, ding,
Sweet lovers love the spring.
(First and Second Pages)

A poor virgin sir, an ill-favoured thing sir, but mine own.
(Touchstone)

Your If is the only peacemaker.
(Touchstone)

If it be true that good wine needs no bush, 'tis true that a good play needs no epilogue.
(Rosalind)

TROILUS AND CRESSIDA

The juxtaposition of essays on *As You Like It* and *Troilus and Cressida* is entirely deliberate: the one being ultimately resplendent in good will and bonhomie all round; the other demonstrating, almost wholly cynically, the squalor and turpitude of human behaviour. There are positives to be taken from *Troilus and Cressida,* as we shall see, but by and large the overwhelming mood of the play is one of disillusionment at human nature as sulking, selfishness, arrogance, lechery and betrayal dominate at the (potential) expense of honour and love. No resemblance to the shared joys of *As You Like It.* Of course this capacity – what Keats called "negative capability" – to see things from all perspectives is one of the distinguishing features of Shakespeare's genius. It enables the establishment to hail him as 'one of us'[31], whereas those of us of a subversive bent can delight in lords of misrule like Falstaff and in a "snapper-up of unconsidered trifles" like Autolycus in *A Winter's Tale.*

The siege of Troy is one hell of a story. Writers onwards from Homer's *Iliad* have, through the centuries, been attracted to it. Way back towards the end of the 1380s Chaucer wrote *Troilus and Criseyde,* based on Boccaccio's *Il Filostrato* and, most recently, we have seen Caroline Alexander's splendid *The War That Killed Achilles* (2011) and Madeline Miller's Orange Prize winner *The Song of Achilles* (2012). Obviously there have been many other plunderings of the *Iliad* in the years in between too! The main themes of *Troilus and Cressida* are fundamental to human life: fidelity and betrayal in love; honour and dishonour in battle; order – and lack of order – with regard to a functioning society. Material for politicians – and for all of us – to

31   *One Of Us* is the title of Hugo Young's acclaimed biography of Margaret Thatcher, and refers to her belief that society could be divided into two – those who embraced her conservative, establishment values and the rest of us, who could not be trusted.

ponder on.

This is the story. In Troy, Troilus loves Cressida, and through the contrivances of her uncle, Pandarus, they make love and swear eternal fidelity. However, Cressida's father Calchas, a priest, has defected to the Greeks, and he persuades the Greeks to exchange a captured Trojan prisoner for his daughter. Cressida, once she is with the Greeks, becomes Diomedes' mistress, and her infidelity is watched by Troilus in the company of Ulysses. This energises Troilus into fighting ferociously the next day. The war has in fact been dragging on for seven years and a certain lethargy has set in on both sides. Achilles has not received sufficient deference from Agamemnon and so sulks in his tent with his lover Patroclus. The most valiant and honourable of all the warriors, the Trojan Hector, fights Ajax in single combat but, as he is a relative, refuses to kill him. Eventually, though, he gets his wish to fight the Greeks' greatest warrior Achilles, as Achilles is stirred into action by Hector killing his friend Patroclus. Hector is then killed deceitfully and his body disgraced. As the "deformed and scurrilous Greek" Thersites – who, with Pandarus, acts as a commentator on the action – says: "Lechery, lechery; still wars and lechery; nothing else holds fashion."

Lechery, of course, is at the heart of the Trojan War. We do not need the words of the "rank" Thersites, a self-confessed "rascal, a scurvy railing knave, very filthy rogue", for this. Whether we accept the school of thought that sees Paris as a forcible abductor of Helen or whether we prefer to believe that Helen left Menelaus for Paris willingly – and Shakespeare in *Troilus and Cressida* is fairly equivocal on the subject and indeed does not really concern himself with the issue – it is indisputable that lechery, sexual desire, is at the root of the Greco/Trojan conflict. Menelaus has been cuckolded and Troilus describes Helen as "a pearl whose price has launched above a thousand ships". Even when Pandarus is joking with Cassandra about how Helen thought Troilus more attractive than Paris, there is agreement about the beauty of Helen. Paris has not the slightest intention to return Helen, though his father points out that "...you speak / Like one besotted on your sweet delights. / You have the honey still, but these the gall."

Paris, though, believes that honourably keeping Helen will wipe off "the soil of her fair rape". Hector actually gets to the nub of the moral debate when he talks of Helen being the wife of Sparta's king which means that "these moral laws / Of nature and of nations speak aloud / To have her back returned", but then he cops out of this moral line by urging the keeping of Helen "for 'tis a cause that hath no mean dependence / Upon our joint and several dignities". The lecherous love of Paris and Helen – "war for a placket" (petticoat) – are Thersites' words for it; but this is not the focus of the play: it simply triggers the action. But Shakespeare does give us two pictures of lovers: Achilles and Patroclus, and Troilus and Cressida.

Let us consider Troilus and Cressida. The play's audience is never in any doubt that Troilus loves Cressida: "I am mad in Cressid's love." And when they come together in Act 3 Scene 2 Troilus is initially "bereft of all words". Before their love is consummated, too, we hear of Troilus being the yardstick for all future generations by which to measure truth and constancy in love. Even when Cressida betrays him, Troilus' love does not waver. Perhaps there was a warning in Cressida's uncle having to serve as a pimp before they could get together: "I cannot come to Cressid but by Pandar," bewails Troilus at the outset of the play. Not a good omen for a relationship.

It is with Cressida, though, that the ignominy of failing to honour love's vows falls: "frailty thy name is woman" – Hamlet's comment on his mother is at least equally applicable to Cressida. Cressida is much more interesting than Troilus, who is little more than a lovesick youth. Our first encounter with her sees her cracking jokes with a companion and immediately after she is joshing with her uncle Pandarus, who is trying to claim the superiority of Troilus to Hector and, briefly, to Achilles: "pull the other one" is her basic response to this. Yet when left alone she admits her attraction to Troilus and explains why she is holding off: "Things won are done, joy's soul lies in the doing." And when she and Troilus are together she confesses: "I was won, my lord, with the first glance", and they leave for a bed to "press to death".

If that were all we would be celebrating a happy love affair. In the quite lengthy encounter that concludes with the bed-pressing, Cressida has already expressed doubts about the inadequacy of men's performance when contrasted to their boasts; she is ashamed that she has taken the lead in seeming to beg for a kiss; she has expressed the view that wisdom and love are incompatible; and in declaring her love for Troilus she has said that if she ever is false her name should become a byword for infidelity. After they have spent their only night together, after much crude lip-smacking from Pandarus, Cressida does complain that the night has been too brief and that "you men will never tarry". However, when confronted with her being part of a prisoner exchange with Antenor so that she can rejoin her father who had defected to the Greek camp, she disses her relationship with her father, claiming that "no soul near me / As the sweet Troilus", and cries out, with consummate irony: "O you gods divine, / Make Cressid's name the very crown of falsehood / If ever she leave Troilus."

In fact, with very little heart-searching, she abandons Troilus and gives herself to Diomedes, who was the Greek go-between in the exchanging of Antenor for Cressida. Perhaps her more complex take on the nature of relationships, which I outlined above, is indicative of a mind that will not yield to simple answers and simple professions of love; perhaps her quick-wittedness indicates a liveliness of mind, able to respond with intelligence to changed situations; perhaps she realizes on which side her bread will now be buttered; perhaps she sees the warrior Diomedes, full of sexual bravado in their first meeting, and contrasts him with the adolescent Troilus. Whatever the reason, despite her continued iterations of being true to Troilus, she has few qualms about being bedded by Diomedes. It is interesting too that on her arrival at the Greek camp all the generals take it in turn to kiss her, with the exception of Ulysses, who scorns her, claiming to see her true character:

> *Her wanton spirits look out*
> *At every joint and motive of her body…*
> *…set them down*
> *For sluttish spoils of opportunity*
> *And daughters of the game.*

This assessment of Ulysses' I think has to be taken seriously; he, together with Hector, is the voice of good sense and reason in *Troilus and Cressida*. Seeing/reading the play we notice Cressida's vitality;

we recognize a certain complexity of thought. In the last words we hear her speak, Cressida acknowledges this:

> *Troilus, farewell. One eye looks on thee,*
> *But with my heart the other eye doth see.*
> *Ah, poor our sex! this fault I find,*
> *The error of our eye directs our mind.*

Thersites interprets this as her saying "My mind is now turned whore." Complex and interesting Cressida certainly is, but she also epitomizes a very real cynicism about love which Shakespeare presents in *Troilus and Cressida*.

There **is** an example of a secure relationship in *Troilus and Cressida* and that is in the liaison between Achilles and Patroclus. We initially hear of Achilles lolling on his "lazy bed" with Patroclus, while Patroclus slanders the Greek generals by grotesquely parodying them. Thersites – a commentator prone to exaggeration but nonetheless able to perceive the kernel of truth in most situations – labels Patroclus Achilles' "brach" (bitch) and "masculine whore", and thinks that if it were left to Achilles and Patroclus the walls of Troy will stand "till they fall of themselves". Ulysses' taunt a little later that Achilles is in love with Hector's sister Polyxena, and that it would befit Achilles to throw down Hector rather than his sister, whether it be true or not[32], neither diminishes nor negates the relationship between Achilles and Patroclus. Greek relationships were not exclusively with one person or with one sex.

Up until this Polyxena moment Achilles is boastfully content: "fortune and I are friends," he says. (Agamemnon and Ulysses have been trying to persuade Achilles to take up arms against the Trojans, and against Hector in particular, by setting up Ajax as the Greeks' greatest warrior, hoping this will sufficiently rile Achilles into action. The ploy had not worked.) Initially Patroclus responds to the Polyxena taunt by blaming himself for Achilles being loathed as "… an effeminate man in time of action: / They think my little stomach to the war / And your great love to me restrains you thus".

---

32   Achilles mentions this 'love' for Polyxena later when referring to a letter he has received from Queen Hecuba, so it does seem real enough and Achilles professes it to be a major motivating factor.

"Sweet, rouse yourself," he advises his lover, and Achilles recognizes – at last – that his reputation is at stake. With this in mind Achilles drinks with Hector as friends the night before what is to be a fatal battle, promising to meet him tomorrow "fell[33] as death". But even with that promise made, the battle on the morrow has already been waging quite a while before Achilles enters it – and what causes him eventually to fight? The death of his friend/lover Patroclus in battle. Ulysses is able to encourage the Greek fighters with the words: "O, courage, courage, princes! Great Achilles / Is arming, weeping, cursing, vowing vengeance. / Patroclus' wounds have roused his drowsy blood."

So, unlike that of Menelaus and Helen and that of Troilus and Cressida, we do have a relationship which endures to the death in *Troilus and Cressida*: that of Achilles and Patroclus. This most cynical of plays does have positive values and there would be even more positivity if, fired by the death of Patroclus, Achilles were to go on to amazing feats of valour and heroism. Alas, no! Hector is indeed killed and by Achilles, but it is an unarmed Hector, believing his day's work is done and resting after battle, that Achilles comes across and, despite Hector's plea that he should forego his advantage, kills. And then, not content with that lack of chivalry, Hector's body is tied to the tail of Achilles' horse and is ignominiously dragged around the walls of Troy. That is the last action of the play, which concludes with Agamemnon's assumption that the Greeks will now take Troy, Troilus thinking that hopes of revenge will hide the Trojans' inner woe and calling Achilles a "great-sized coward". Finally, Pandarus, in the very last words of the play, bequeaths the audience his venereal diseases!

Hector and Troilus come out of the battle scenes quite well, but no one else does. Indeed, Achilles not only kills an unarmed Hector, but previously had instructed his soldiers, his Myrmidons, to surround Hector and allow him no escape once he had been found. And it is not just that "combat trauma undoes character" as Caroline Alexander writes in *The War that Killed Achilles*, for Shakespeare has already given us disconcertingly unattractive portraits of many of the Greek and Trojan generals when off the battlefield. The mocking

---

33   Fell = fierce.

tone of *Troilus and Cressida* is set from the outset, when Cressida is seen commenting on the Greek warriors as they return from the battle and when Pandarus calls Achilles "a very camel". Neither what one imagines the combatants would call deeds of derring-do nor their perpetrators are being taken seriously. Honour and renown are not present. Ulysses' plan to get Achilles involved in the fighting involves pushing Ajax to the fore as (after Achilles) acknowledgedly the best Greek warrior, but Ulysses describes him as "blockish" and "brainless". And when we meet Ajax he is exchanging insults (and losing the contest) with Thersites and then physically beating him. He asks from Agamemnon, and receives, assurances of his superiority to Achilles, and then wholly unaware of any contradiction insists that he does not know what pride is and that "I do hate a proud man." Ulysses comments that if all men were like Ajax "wit would be out of fashion".

Yet Ajax is the second most valiant Greek, and Achilles, the greatest fighter of all, has behaved despicably towards Hector. The Greek army, in fact, is given a pretty bad press by Shakespeare. It's not just these two: the ten-year stretch of war is on behalf of the cuckolded Menelaus, Diomedes (and indeed all the Greek generals) sexually bully Cressida as soon as they meet her, and, if we go back to the launching of the argosy that set sail for Troy, the lack of wind for the sails was alleviated only by Agamemnon's sacrifice of his daughter Iphigenia to the gods. A moral bankruptcy pervades the Greek camp.

But we cannot say that this is evidence of Shakespeare scorning the possibility of honour existing in times of war: Falstaff's behaviour in *King Henry IV Part 2* and his dicta that "honour is a mere scutcheon"[34] and that "the better part of valour is discretion" attest to a similar mode of thinking to that of *Troilus and Cressida*, but then Shakespeare also writes *King Henry V* and, notwithstanding the behaviour of Pistol, Bardolph and Nym, that play, with its Harfleur and Agincourt speeches, leaves us with a powerful taste of the glory and honour to be gained from a patriotic war. Shakespeare sees it all. His perspectives are multiple.

---

34   A scutcheon is the shield on which a coat of arms is painted, and is associated with funerals, for it was carried to church and then hung on the church wall after a warrior's death.

To return to *Troilus and Cressida,* where it is true that, although the emphasis is not on them, the Trojans do appear more honourable than the Greeks. What, though, of Ulysses? He is twice pivotal to the action, in so far as it is he who devises the plan, vis-à-vis Ajax, to jolt Achilles into fighting, and he also accompanies Troilus to the tent of Diomedes and shows him Cressida's infidelity. Much more than this, though, Shakespeare presents Ulysses as the voice of wisdom and gives him the two most memorable speeches in the play. The first one is about "the specialty of rule hath been neglected", in which he argues that each thing in the universe has its place and that each person has his degree, and once people ignore their place in society and disdain their superiors discord inevitably follows. He puts the blame firmly on Achilles for not showing respect, with the result that people are discontented and critical of their superiors, so that "Troy in our weakness stands, not in her strength." It is an argument with which the establishment of any country would concur. It could be included in any Conservative party statement of beliefs, and indeed was an argument used when *That Was the Week That Was* began in 1964. Stay in your allotted stratum of society and respect your betters. Do not contemplate any ideas above your station. Ulysses said it all in *Troilus and Cressida.*

Ulysses' other big speech in the play is about time. He speaks it to Achilles, arguing that good deeds are soon forgotten and that "perseverance keeps honour bright". Everything – and I have quoted this section of the speech in the Memorable Quotations section – is lost to or destroyed by time, which is why one has to live and act in the present – an existential point, and one which appears to change the thinking of both Patroclus and Achilles. Both these speeches are food for political and philosophical discussion.

These speeches of Ulysses are very long and one can perhaps understand why Dryden, when rewriting *Troilus and Cressida,* shortened the council scenes of both the Greeks and the Trojans (though not why he made Cressida faithful to the end!). These council scenes are long scenes and an audience can (and sometimes does) get restive. No, it is not an easy play, and, I am reliably told, it is a play universally hated by present-day undergraduate Cambridge students who have to know and comment on its many different textual readings in its two Quartos.

I have no doubt, however, that *Troilus and Cressida* is a play which yields a good deal to 21st century thinking. There is no record of any performances of it between 1734 and 1898, but after the First World War it has become increasingly popular. Why? It captures a mood of disillusionment: hierarchies are not to be trusted, honour can be bought and loved ones can be snatched away indiscriminately. Respect and deference cannot be enjoined – they have to be earned, and indeed deference is in itself a questionable attitude. All these issues make this play worthy of visiting.

Michael Long[35] writes of the "sardonic laughter" which permeates *Troilus and Cressida*, and it is laughter at a profound dislocation of values. Thersites, Pandarus, Cressida, Ajax, Achilles and Diomedes are all main characters whose morality is to say the least suspect. Yet, to conclude on a slightly upbeat note, there is in the play an acknowledgment of the motivating power of love as both Troilus and Achilles go into battle for the sake of love. And the play is called *Troilus and Cressida*, and although the twenty-three year old Troilus may behave like an adolescent, he is virtuous! What a play!

---

35   In *The Unnatural Scene*, Methuen 1976.

Memorable Quotations From *Troilus and Cressida*

He that will have a cake out of the wheat must tarry the grinding.
(Pandarus)

...she's a merry Greek indeed.
(Cressida)

Women are angels, wooing;
Things won are done, joy's soul lies in the doing...
Men prize the thing ungained more than it is.
(Cressida)

The specialty of rule hath been neglected...
The heavens themselves, the planets and this centre
Observe degree, priority, and place...
Take but degree away, untune that string,
And hark what discord follows.
(Ulysses)

Let us, like merchants,
First show foul wares, and think perchance they'll sell...
(Ulysses)

You fur your gloves with reason... Reason and respect
Make livers pale and lustihood deject.
(Troilus)

You have the honey still, but these the gall...
(Priam)

Young men, whom Aristotle thought
Unfit to hear moral philosophy.
(Hector)

The vengeance on the whole camp! or, rather, the Neapolitan bone-ache, for that, methinks, is the curse depending on those who war for a placket.
(Thersites)

Is love a generation of vipers?
(Pandarus)

Sweet, above thought I love thee.
(Paris)

This is the monstrosity in love, lady, that the will is infinite and the execution confined; that the desire is boundless and the act a slave to limit.
(Troilus)
They say all lovers swear more performance than they are able.
(Cressida)

...to be wise and love
Exceeds man's might; that dwells with gods above.
(Cressida)

Let all constant men be Troiluses, all false women Cressidas, and all brokers-between Pandars.
(Pandarus)

Time hath, my lord, a wallet at his back,
Wherein he puts alms for oblivion,
A great-sized monster of ingratitudes...
Perseverance, dear my lord,
Keeps honour bright... Let not virtue seek
Remuneration for the thing it was. For beauty, wit,
High birth, vigour of bone, desert in service,
Love, friendship, charity, are subjects all
To envious and calumniating time.
(Ulysses)

A woman impudent and mannish grown
Is not more loathed than an effeminate man
In time of action.
(Patroclus)

O you gods divine,
Make Cressid's name the very crown of falsehood
If ever she leave Troilus.
(Cressida)

'Tis but early days.
(Achilles)

There's language in her eye, her cheek, her lip;
Nay, her foot speaks. Her wanton spirits look out
At every joint and motive of her body... set them down
For sluttish spoils of opportunity
And daughters of the game.
(Ulysses)

Let me embrace thee, good old chronicle,
That hast so long walked hand in hand with time.
(Hector to Nestor)

The end crowns all,
And that old arbitrator, Time,
Will one day end it.
(Hector)

But still sweet love is food for fortune's tooth.
(Troilus)

Troilus, farewell. One eye yet looks on thee,
But with my heart the other eye doth see.
Ah, poor our sex! this fault in us I find,
The error of our eye directs our mind.
(Cressida)

Lechery, lechery; still wars and lechery; nothing else holds fashion.
(Thersites)

Words, words, mere words, no matter from the heart.
(Troilus)

THE WINTER'S TALE

If the only Shakespeare play I were to write about was *Troilus and Cressida* I would be giving a totally wrong impression of Shakespeare's work. Of course it is important to show the clay feet of heroes, the infidelity of women and Machiavellian schemes – impropriety and disillusionment everywhere. In a world where we have a British Prime Minister and his Chancellor of the Exchequer squirreling millions of pounds away in their offshore accounts to avoid paying taxes and having the gall to claim that "We are all in this together"; where someone seen by much of the world as a war criminal struts and postures his way around the Middle East as a peace envoy; where a US President orders one drone attack after another, apparently not caring about 'collateral damage', i.e. the deaths of innocent citizens – in such a world the excesses of *Troilus and Cressida* have their place. But just as the three things I have mentioned are not indicative of everything that is happening in the modern world, so Shakespeare depicts values other than those riddling *Troilus and Cressida*.

Which is why I have chosen *The Winter's Tale* as the next play to consider: I see it as a kind of antidote to *Troilus and Cressida*. At the most extreme level there is a contrast between the ultra-realism of *Troilus and Cressida* and the quasi-supernatural, magical ending of *The Winter's Tale*. But throughout the play we have examples of love, honesty, courage, fidelity, forgiveness and reconciliation – ultimately joy abounds. It is the London Olympics 2012 as opposed to the disasters in Iraq and Afghanistan. But just as despite the overall cynicism of *Troilus and Cressida* there are instances of love and courage within the play, so, in reverse, amidst the positivity of *The Winter's Tale* there are instances of negativity: the tinker Autolycus, for example, is not to be trusted, but he does bring a joy and lightness to the stage and is very much a loveable rogue.

No, more significantly, with regard to the darkness within mankind and within *The Winter's Tale*, is the jealousy of Leontes. It is not a scheming and sustained darkness like that of Iago in *Othello*, but once it leaps inescapably to the forefront of Leontes' mind it is deep, destructive and devastating. Within the parameters of a play bringing joy through forgiveness, reconciliation, pure young love and Time, there is very much a large tranche of disturbing psychological realism.

This, then, is the story. Leontes and Polixenes, respectively kings of Sicilia and Bohemia, have been close friends since childhood. Polixenes has been visiting Sicilia for nine months and when Leontes perceives that his very pregnant wife Hermione is being excessively friendly with Polixenes he jumps to the conclusion that Polixenes is the father of the soon-to-be-born child. He orders his servant Camillo to poison Polixenes, but Camillo alerts Polixenes to Leontes' thinking and the two escape to Bohemia. In Sicilia Hermione is denounced, her baby is taken away from her and, despite everyone's protestations of Hermione's innocence (and especially those of Hermione herself and her faithful servant Paulina), she is threatened with the sentence of death but then reportedly dies of natural causes – as does the other child of Leontes and Hermione, Mamillius. Initially Leontes refuses to believe the Delphic Oracle pronouncing Hermione's innocence but later is mortified and repents. Before the repentance, however, Paulina's husband, Antigonus, has been entrusted to leave Hermione's baby girl on a mountain side; he does this, in Bohemia, but then is eaten by a bear. The child, called Perdita ('the lost girl'), is taken in and brought up by a shepherd. Sixteen years later, Florizel, the son of Polixenes, while hunting across the aforementioned shepherd's land, has seen Perdita and fallen in love with her. When Polixenes finds out, he disapproves of his son and his love for the common shepherdess. (This happens in Act 4, which is also notable for the bucolic festivities of a sheep-shearing feast and the character of Autolycus.) However, everyone eventually comes together at the Sicilian court, where it is revealed that Hermione is not dead: she (apparently magically) comes to life and is reconciled with Leontes, who is also reconciled with Polixenes. Paulina is given a new husband in the form of Camillo, and of course, Florizel and Perdita will be happily married. Harmony all round.

Such is *The Winter's Tale*, bearing no relation to David Essex's forlorn song – *A Winter's Tale* – of the 1960s, telling of "one more love that's failed". I see the title of the play as a throwaway, not particularly significant title, referring to Mamillius' intent to tell the court ladies a nerve-jangling story of sprites and goblins and churchyards, which he introduces with the words: "A sad tale's best for winter." Maybe that is meant as an almost subliminal preparation for the mysterious, magical world with which the play ends, or maybe not. But undoubtedly that comment is the source of Shakespeare's titling the play.

Yet Mamillius talks of a "sad tale" and I am extolling the virtues of this play as being those of reconciliation and harmony, which I think should be at the forefront of all political discourse. How much sadness is there to be found in *The Winter's Tale*? We the audience bridle with indignation at the injustice that is done to Hermione and are saddened by her apparent death and the fate of her two children. I would argue, though, that we know from the beginning that death and destruction are not the themes of *The Winter's Tale*. Leontes is in a minority of one in believing in Hermione's infidelity and his being cuckolded: his jealousy of Polixenes, based on his closeness with Hermione, exhibited by such behaviour as their "paddling palms", "leaning cheek to cheek" and "kissing with inside lip", is one of a sudden, intemperate flaring up. Such flames can easily be doused unless they are fed constantly with more fuel, as Iago does to Othello. Shakespeare presents it to us as jealousy almost on impulse, although it should be remembered that Polixenes has already stayed nine months in Sicilia and, in my experience, most house guests are welcome for two days, which might sometimes be stretched to three days. (After that…) And nine months?!

Be that as it may, when seeing the play we are confident that Leontes will, with an alacrity equal to that with which he leaped to condemn Hermione, realise the folly of that condemnation and regret and repent of his behaviour. And, although jealousy is the unacceptable face of love, it can be – as in this instance – an indication of an extreme form of love. Until this extended stay of Polixenes there is no indication of anything but happiness in the relationship of Leontes and Hermione, so calling Hermione "slippery" and a "hobby-horse" indicates the derangement of Leontes' mind. Of course what is doubly distressing for Leontes is the closeness that had existed between himself and Polixenes: as lads they had been brought up together, "as twinn'd lambs that did frisk i' the sun"; they lived in the present which was "to be boy eternal". Polixenes talks of their innocent friendship and jests about the loss of innocence when their respective queens entered their lives so, as I see it, even if the relationship between Leontes and Polixenes may not have been homosexual, there is every indication of its being homoerotic. Thus once Leontes gets the idea of Polixenes and Hermione being lovers into his mind, he is beset by losing, not just one, but the two people he loves most in the world. No wonder he is devastated, far more than was Elvis Presley, when in what according to Leontes was Polixenes' position, he sang of being "in love with the girl of my best friend".

Thus we have an effective psychological portrait of how jealousy can make a man (and indeed a king) a monster. Unable to rid himself of his torturing fantasies Leontes devastates his own life and very nearly loses his wife, his best friend and his daughter, and he does lose his son. Had his orders been carried out his wife and friend would have been killed and he was so lucky that his baby daughter, left on a mountainside to die, did in fact survive. It would be very difficult to create a more destructive vision of the elemental power of jealousy.

No one could claim that Leontes is a great tragic hero; nor could it be claimed that any profound characterization is to be found elsewhere in *The Winter's Tale*. Once he has heard that his son Mamillius has died Leontes immediately sees this as a result of his profanity against the Delphic Oracle and asks Apollo's forgiveness – there is a sudden volte-face and wish to be reconciled with Hermione and Polixenes. There is no soul-searching, no ongoing internal life explored in soliloquys. Of course there can be no immediate forgiveness for the brutality of his thinking and his orders. He has to be given time – sixteen years in fact – to reflect on and be punished for his offences against love and fidelity. But whereas with someone like Macbeth we are privy to the workings and development of his mind, we are given very little of the internal landscape of Leontes.

The other major characters in *The Winter' Tale* are also not explored in any depth. To some extent they are cyphers as they represent a particular quality, but they are also nonetheless distinctly realised. Leaving aside Autolycus for the moment, I am thinking of Hermione, Paulina and Perdita. Hermione is strong in her protestations of innocence. She is "not prone to weeping" but has a burning grief within, and she maintains her honour before Leontes with calmness, blaming her fate on the temporary reign of some "ill planet", and counsels herself to be patient. As befits the daughter of the Emperor of Russia, Hermione explains with total dignity how she performed her hostess duties to Polixenes as Leontes had commanded and how her love for Leontes and her children was foremost in her life. Very forcefully and convincingly – but not to Leontes – she defends her honour. At the end of the play Hermione addresses Perdita only, asserting that what has kept her alive in hope was the Oracle saying that her daughter lived, and now she wants to hear more about Perdita's survival and life. She addresses not a word to Leontes. In view of the depth of Leontes' repentance for his distrust of Hermione and Polixenes (and in view of the final harmony elsewhere in *The Winter's Tale*) it is extremely likely that Hermione will forgive Leontes, but it is not quite a given and the actress playing Hermione has opportunities for a complex response to her husband.

The response of Paulina is not dissimilar. Her ploy of taking Hermione's newly born baby to Leontes and undertaking the advocacy of Hermione "to th' loud'st", indeed showing him how the baby is a copy of her father, i.e. Leontes, fails and Paulina is threatened (with both hanging and being burned at the stake). Nonetheless Paulina continues to protest the innocence of Hermione and it is she who organises the plan for keeping Hermione alive through bringing news to Leontes of her death, and indeed swearing to her death before the "tyrant". In this first part of the play Paulina pulls no punches in her advocacy for Hermione and her criticism of Leontes' unwarranted behaviour. A bold, strong woman. In the final Act of *The Winter's Tale* it is she who calls for music and for the alleged statue of Hermione to descend and be seen to be alive. She has kept Hermione alive and ministered to her. Paulina is very much a plot agent, but she is so much more than this. No longer calling her "a most intelligencing bawd", she has become, in Leontes' eyes, "the grave and good Paulina", and having lost her husband to a bear in the deserts of Bohemia sixteen years previously, she is rewarded, "old turtle" as she claims to be, with a new husband, the faithful Camillo. That is all part of the harmony and happy ending scenario. For me what is more important to note is that here we have – in contrast to the perfidy and weakness of the women in *Troilus and Cressida* – another strong woman. Unlike Dickens, Shakespeare can portray women as being faithful and strong-minded, passionate in their beliefs but reasonable in their behaviour. In reality, much more than cyphers.

And the same is true of Perdita. There is a certain stoic acceptance in her character as she does not wilt before Polixenes when he reveals himself and is appalled at his son relating to a commoner – appalled to the extent of threatening to have her beauty "scratch'd with briers", calling her a "fresh piece of excellent witchcraft". The outstanding characteristics of Perdita, though, are her beauty, grace and modesty. Of her beauty there is no doubt. Time introduces her as "grown in grace equal with wond'ring" and even old Camillo says he could spend his life just gazing at her. From the time we meet her, bedecked as the goddess Flora at the sheep-shearing feast, there is nothing but grace in her movements and utterances, but it is her modesty that I find the most beguiling and worthy character trait. Right at the outset she expresses how uncomfortable she is as "a poor lowly maid" all dressed up as a goddess, and how she (rightly) fears the reaction of Florizel's father were he to find his son "vilely bound up" with herself, and when Polixenes addresses her as "enchantment" and threatens her with a cruel death if she ever again allows Florizel into her life, she comments on her recent life as being like a dream and immediately and modestly says she will return to milking her ewes. Yes, Perdita says she will weep but there are no protestations of loss and emotional outbursts such as we get from Cleopatra and Juliet. A calm, resigned modesty, indicative of her knowing her place in the social scheme of things. I will, though, leave the last words on the nature of Perdita to Polixenes:

> *This is the prettiest low-born lass that ever*
> *Ran on the green-sward: nothing she does or seems*
> *But smacks of something greater than herself,*
> *Too noble for this place.*

But, until she is revealed to be Leontes and Hermione's daughter,

Perdita is not of the right class for the son of Polixenes. Class is not an easy issue for Shakespeare to deal with, licensed as he was to James I as a "King's Man". I don't think he is making any serious points about it in *The Winter's Tale* but there is some humour to be had at the end of the play when the Shepherd who had brought up Perdita and his Clown son discuss how their behaviour will change "now we are gentlemen". Just as today an aristocrat born to the cause can sniff out any pretentious middle-class person a mile off, so you could say that Shakespeare – while not necessarily endorsing class distinction – is at least saying "once a peasant, always a peasant" and we should keep to our own class. Only love has a chance of breaking down the class barriers...

Which is where Florizel comes in. But, other than to note that, perhaps along with Romeo and Troilus and Ferdinand (in *The Tempest*), he is one of Shakespeare's lovesick young men who try to behave honourably and lovingly, there is little to say about him. He stands up to his father and rejects his inheritance in favour of Perdita, but, unlike Troilus and Romeo, has no traumas to suffer and does not even have to bear the log-carrying burden imposed upon Ferdinand by Prospero before he can romantically approach his daughter Miranda. No, all is – comparatively – sweetness and light, as befits the mood of *The Winter's Tale*, with the young lovers Perdita and Florizel.

There are other themes, though, that warrant at least passing comment before we conclude with a look at Autolycus. Before he reveals his kingly identity, Polixenes has a lengthy discussion with Perdita about hybrids and whether by grafting different plants together man can improve on nature: Polixenes thinks so[36], but Perdita, equating the artificiality of the cross-breeding of plants with women using make-up, stands up strongly for pure breeding. Some have seen this discussion as central to an ongoing issue raised by Shakespeare in a number of his plays about whether art can better nature. Maybe, but it certainly gives Perdita the opportunity to speak lovingly and knowledgeably about flowers – such as "pale primroses / That die

---

36   Logically, one might think that this argument would open up the possibility for Polixenes of his accepting Perdita. But manifestly the class system is for him more important with regard to people than to plants.

unmarried, ere they can behold / Bright Phoebus[37] in his strength".

(There is, though, some confusion as to when exactly Act 4 takes place, seasonally speaking. It is a sheep-shearing festival that we witness, which would place the scene in mid-June, and Perdita indeed regrets that she can no longer give spring flowers to her guests, but she does give flowers of "middle summer" and seems to indicate elsewhere that the time of the year is on the cusp of autumn.)

Be that as it may, what is important is that Perdita has demonstrated her credentials as a girl brought up in the country. So is there a debate within this play about the values of country life as distinct from (and opposed to) the values of the court? Personally I think not – Florizel, for example, was brought up in the court, as was Camillo, and it is difficult to find fault with them. Paulina and Hermione too. There's nothing more to be said.

No, the Arcadian scene is necessary for the plot in that the plot needs time (sixteen years) and space (Bohemia). It would be daft were Perdita to be found in Sicilia three weeks after her removal from the court. Perhaps too the inclusion of a pastoral masque was a response to the current popularity of such events at court.[38] (And the magic at the end of *The Winter's Tale*, when the statue comes to life, would too have appealed to the court of James I with his belief in evil and good spirits – more about this when we come to *Macbeth*.)

Autolycus. "A snapper-up of unconsidered trifles", fearful of beating and hanging in this life and closing his mind to what the life to come might have in store for him. A skilled stealer of sheets left drying on hedgerows, a pickpocket, a cutpurse thief, a trickster of a con artist who runs rings round and robs the simple-minded. A man with an eye for the main chance, always looking after number one. He believes Fortune approves of his dishonesty by dropping "booties in my mouth". A rogue, yes, but an entirely loveable and intelligently quick-witted rogue. Far more of a trickster than a criminal, he brings vitality to *The Winter's Tale* as well as music and laughter.

37   Phoebus is Phoebus Apollo, the god of light, or the sun.
38   Ben Jonson's *Masque of Oberon* had, for example, been performed at court on New Year's Day 1611 – a play in which there was, similarly to *The Winter's Tale* (also 1611), a dance of ten or twelve satyrs.

Once upon a time he served Prince Florizel and was dressed in court velvet but, as a result of gambling and loose women, he is reduced in the world – "a thing of rags and patches", to quote W. S. Gilbert, referring to Nanki-Poo in *The Mikado*[39]. Fundamentally, though, Autolycus is fun: in many ways he resembles Sir John Falstaff, but Falstaff, leading his scarecrow army to their death, together with his own behaviour on the battlefield, is actually culpable of certain heinous acts, whereas in comparison Autolycus is almost blameless. His offences are trivial, and with regard to this we can compare and contrast him with Leontes. The Autolycus of Act 4 is entirely likeable and memorable.

We receive good cheer from Autolycus, just as we receive good cheer from *The Winter's Tale*. I am aware that I have been extolling the virtues of *The Winter's Tale* as a feel-good, harmonious play, yet up to the end of Act 3 the storyline reads more like a tragedy. I would argue that such is Leontes' obviously outrageous behaviour, presenting a perspective not shared by anyone else in the play, that this betokens that there has to be a movement from that situation towards something more positive, and the survival of Perdita reinforces this. We know that Leontes' position is untenable. What is needed is Time. It is no coincidence that Robert Greene's play *Pandosto*, on which *The Winter's Tale* is based, was subtitled *The Triumph of Time*. We need time to repent, we need time to forgive and we need time to ensure the reality of a true harmony. And it is true harmony that *The Winter's Tale* is working towards, and which is achieved in the end. It is good to know that this is a possibility, especially after the horrors of *Troilus and Cressida*!

---

39   Gilbert's line being a perversion of Hamlet's description of his murdering uncle as "a king of shreds and patches".

Memorable Quotations From *The Winter's Tale*

Two lads that thought there was no more behind,
But such a day tomorrow as today,
And to be boy eternal.
(Polixenes)

You may ride's
With one soft kiss a thousand furlongs ere
With spur we heat an acre.
(Hermione)

To mingle friendship far, is mingling bloods...
...to be paddling palms and pinching fingers...
...Still virginalling
Upon his palm.
(Leontes)

He makes a July's day short as December.
(Polixenes)

There have been... cuckolds ere now
And many a man there is... holds his wife by th' arm,
That little thinks she has been sluic'd in's absence
And his pond fish'd by his next neighbour, by
Sir Smile, his neighbour... Should all despair
That have revolted wives, the tenth of mankind
Would hang themselves...
It is a bawdy planet...
(Leontes)

Is whispering nothing?
Is leaning cheek to cheek? is meeting noses?
Kissing with inside lip?
(Leontes)

A sad tale's best for winter.
(Mamillius)

It is an heretic that makes the fire,
Not she which burns in it.
(Paulina)

You speak a language that I understand not:
My life stands in the level of your dreams...
(Hermione)

I do refer me to the Oracle:
Apollo be my judge!
(Hermione)

I am a feather for each wind that blows.
(Leontes)

Exit, pursued by a bear.
(Stage direction)

I would there were no age between ten and three-and-twenty, or that youth
would sleep out the rest; for there is nothing in the between but getting
wenches with child, wronging the ancientry, stealing, fighting...
(Shepherd)

Thou met'st with things dying, I with things new-born.
(Shepherd)

I that please some, try all.
(Time)

When daffodils begin to peer,
With heigh! the doxy over the dale,
Why then come in the sweet o' the year,
For the red blood reigns in the winter's pale.
The white sheeting bleaching on the hedge,
With hey! the sweet birds, O how they sing!
Doth set my pugging tooth on edge;
For a quart of ale is a dish for a king.
(Autolycus)

My father named me Autolycus; who, being as I am, littered under Mercury,
was likewise a snapper-up of unconsidered trifles… beating and hanging
are terrors to me: for the life to come, I sleep out the thought of it.
(Autolycus)

These are flowers
Of middle summer, and I think they are given
To men of middle age.
(Perdita)

And indeed, sir, there are cozeners abroad; therefore it behoves men to be
wary.
(Autolycus)

Being now awake, I'll queen it no inch further,
But milk my ewes, and weep.
(Perdita)

Ha, ha! what a fool Honesty is! and Trust, his sworn brother, a very simple
gentleman!
(Autolycus)

A good nose is requisite also, to smell out work for the other senses.
(Autolycus)

Though I am not naturally honest, I am so sometimes by chance… Let me
have no lying: it becomes none but tradesmen.
(Autolycus)

Music, awake her; strike!
(Music)
'Tis time; descend; be stone no more; approach...
(Paulina)

If this be magic, let it be an art
Lawful as eating.
(Leontes)

OTHELLO

There are major issues of race, law and government raised in *Othello* but what elevates it to great heights are the characterisation and psychological insights that Shakespeare reveals and explores. Iago – along with Cleopatra, Lear, Falstaff and Hamlet – is one of Shakespeare's outstanding characterisations, but Othello and Desdemona are both also fully realised. Together with a fullness of minor characters – Roderigo, Emilia, Bianca, Brabantio and Cassio for example – who are similarly individuated, they constitute a gallery of fascinating people, demonstrating yet again the insight and understanding Shakespeare had of the processes of the human mind and its consequences. Being made increasingly aware of our common humanity and its weaknesses is, of course, valuable for all of us, but if pragmatic politicians want more, the difficult issues of loyalty and preferment are highlighted and are manifestly not irrelevant to the unseen consequences of cabinet shuffles. And the Duke of Venice provides an excellent example of decisive crisis management.

The first Act of *Othello* takes place in Venice. Iago, an experienced and hitherto loyal military colleague of his commanding officer Othello, has been passed over for preferment and a mere inexperienced theoretician, Cassio, is to be Othello's second in command, his lieutenant. Iago vows revenge on Othello. His first act of betrayal is, by exploiting Roderigo's infatuation for Desdemona, to inform Desdemona's father that his daughter has eloped with Othello. Othello is in fact about to be sent to Cyprus by the Venetian state to organise resistance to what is seen as a large Turkish invasion. Brabantio, Desdemona's father, remains horrified by the thought of sex between his white daughter and the black Moor, but Othello and Desdemona explain fully their love for each other and Othello – together with Cassio and Iago and Desdemona – carries on with the state business and sails for Cyprus.

The last four Acts are in Cyprus. There has been a terrific storm and, although the Venetian ships arrive safely at harbour, the Turkish fleet has been destroyed, so there is no longer a threat of invasion. Basically, Iago plays on Othello's insecurity. He suggests that Cassio is having an affair with Desdemona, and having acquired the sobriquet of "honest", Iago's villainy is not suspected. With the help of Roderigo, for whom Iago has promised to secure the love of Desdemona, he contrives to get Cassio drunk and involved in a brawl. The outcome of this is that Cassio loses his job – and Desdemona's appealing for the reinstatement of Cassio only fuels Othello's insecurity and jealousy. Tormented, and totally unreasonably believing that Desdemona is free with her sexual bounty, Othello decides to kill her and indeed suffocates her. It is Emilia, Iago's wife and maidservant to Desdemona, who, knowing the complete innocence of Desdemona and suddenly realising what her husband has been doing, makes sense of it all and denounces her husband, who then stabs her to death. Roderigo has already been killed (for he knew too much) by Iago, and now Othello, understanding his folly, takes his own life. Iago resolves that he will never speak another word, and Cassio, on orders from Venice, is given the Governorship of Cyprus.

That's the story. What about the characters? Othello is the title character: the Moor of Venice, based on an original story by the Italian writer Cinthio, and described in the Dramatis Personae by later editors of the play – though not by Shakespeare – as "a noble Moor in the service of the Venetian state". As readers/spectators there are scenes in the middle of the play, though, when we struggle to see his nobility. There is, however, no doubt about his nobility in the opening scenes. He has seen action, some of it amazing, in the service of Venice; he has splendid stories to tell, stories which enthral Desdemona and cause her to fall in love with him. The Duke has total faith in his ability to deal with the potential threat to Cyprus from a Turkish invasion. Othello speaks modestly and measuredly and immediately stops a threatening brawl between Brabantio's entourage and his own: "Keep up your bright swords, for the dew will rust 'em." In his final speech of the play we are again reminded of his dignity and of his service to the state when he wishes there to be an accurate account of his life – "speak to me as I am".

But in between these two scenes we witness a progressively disintegrating Othello. In this last speech Othello describes himself as "one that loved not wisely, but too well; / ...one not easily jealous, but, being wrought, / Perplexed in the extreme". And there is little doubt that Othello does experience, in Iago's words, "the green-ey'd[40] monster" that is jealousy. He cannot bear the pictures that swim into his mind of Desdemona having sex with anyone else: such pictures torture and torment him. It is in particular her relationship with Cassio which Iago insinuatingly dangles before him that brings about the chaos in Othello's mind. And, of course, Cassio is Desdemona's social equal, whereas Othello comes from a different culture and socially is an outsider to Venetian society. It is easy for Iago to prey on Othello's insecurity:

In Venice they do let God see the pranks
They dare not show their husbands.

According to Iago adultery is rife in Venice! And the love that Othello thought he had with Desdemona is thereby sullied. So it is jealousy and insecurity that undermine Othello. To that we can perhaps add credulity, for he fails to question adequately what Iago is doing: his inclination is to believe every word that "honest, honest Iago" says, rather than the protestations of innocence of Desdemona.

There is also the factor that Othello is amazed that Desdemona loves him. Venetian society is manifestly unhappy about the black man marrying into white society: Iago taunts Brabantio[41] with the words: "Even now, very now, an old black ram / Is tupping your white ewe." There is a sexual disgust there and Brabantio can believe only that Othello has used drugs and magic to win Desdemona. Roderigo refers to Othello as "thick lips" and we hear of his "sooty bosom".

---

40   In Verdi's opera *Othello* it is interesting that the green-ey'd monster line is omitted – perhaps because of Verdi's sensitivity about his own name. Verdi's *Othello* has action only in Cyprus – the first Act, in Venice, is omitted.

41   Brabantio's departing comment to Othello: "Look to her, Moor, have a quick eye to see: / She has deceiv'd her father, may do thee" cannot but also help to undermine Othello's confidence.

Indeed one of the ways in which Cassio keeps Roderigo hanging on with the hope of one day winning Desdemona for himself is that she will tire of having sex with an older, uglier and less mannered man and turn to a man of refinement rather than one who will make her vomit! Iago is talking of Cassio as that man of refinement, but the point is that there is acknowledgedly a belief that Othello is, with Desdemona, out of his depth.

Shakespeare is a chronicler of his times and there was what today we would call racist attitudes towards 'blackamoors'[42] in Elizabethan and Jacobean England. Expulsion Orders had been made on all "negars and blackamoors" in 1596 and again in 1601. Elizabethans believed that black people were taking away jobs from native Englishman. In fact only approximately 0.5% of the population was black and they were employed to slave away at the most thankless and menial jobs: the Expulsion Orders were a populist move and not acted on. Parallels with today abound.

But, as ever, Shakespeare is widening contemporary thinking. He had begun to do this with his portrait of Aaron in *Titus Andronicus* some dozen years earlier. Not that black-hearted Aaron is guiltless and he does commit many appalling crimes, but he is shown to be literate and well-read in the classics; to be able, counter to the accepted perception of black people at the time, to exercise a degree of sexual restraint and also to exhibit paternal love. Aaron is human, and Othello even more so. By the end of the play Othello has killed Desdemona, "the sweetest innocent that e'er did lift up eye", yet Shakespeare has enlisted our sympathies for him. We have seen how Iago has manipulated Othello's insecurity; we have been privy to the workings of Othello's mind; we have seen his loss of honour and reputation and his disintegration and descent into chaos. He is a victim. Shakespeare has demonstrated his dignity and stature at the start of *Othello* and he regains it with his closing speech. What a fall was there! And what a sympathetic portrait of love-besotted, credulous, jealous humanity Shakespeare has given us. The Moor of Venice.

---

42   The blanket name 'blackamoor' covered three kinds of black people in the England of the time: domestic slaves, freedmen and Moors. Moors were seen as being in the highest social category.

Desdemona is not a complex character. She is a strong, determined woman, fully aware that she has violated all conventional standards of Venetian decency by marrying Othello, and is prepared to stand up and publicly explain what she has done: the epithet "warrior" given to her by her military husband would seem appropriate. And, of course, she is indisputably in love with Othello – not for his looks, she is at pains to point out: she loved him for his magnificent stories of hardship and derring-do and the pity in her that they evoked, and "saw Othello's visage in his mind", i.e. his black face might have been repulsive but she responded to the quality of his inner being, his mind. But she wants his body too. Her father may see her as a not very bold, still and quiet maiden, but Desdemona is much more of a mature, passionate woman than he has been prepared to acknowledge: she wants to live with the Moor and is determined not to be left behind when Othello sails to Cyprus for, were that to happen, "the rites for which I love him are bereft me". In a vain attempt to win her husband back to his wonted affection towards the end of the play, Desdemona gives instructions to Emilia: "tonight lay on my bed my wedding sheets". It is Othello who, well aware of the mood of sexual horror that accompanies his match with Desdemona, asserts that he does not want her "to please the palate of my appetite", the sexual heat of when he was young having long gone, but "to be free and bounteous of her mind". Desdemona, though, wants all of him. Perhaps it is an error to continue pleading for Cassio's reinstatement but only a serious error in the context of Iago's having sown doubts about the relationship between the ladies' man Cassio and herself. Otherwise it is difficult to find fault with a brave, determined and loving Desdemona.

None of the revulsion about sex comes from Desdemona: Iago and Othello are the culprits. Marilyn French[43] labels the sexual imagery – "the beast with two backs" and "an old black ram tupping your white ewe", for example – "bestial, vicious and chaotic". Iago fears that Othello has slept with his wife Emilia, Othello conjures up pictures of Desdemona having group sex with the pioneers[44] in his army, and Iago tortures him with the picture of Cassio in bed with Desdemona, laying his leg over her thigh. Female infidelity torments

43   *Shakespeare's Division of Experience* (1982).
44   Pioneers were the lowest, most menial soldiers: they dug in the mud.

insecure male minds.

Iago too is very critical of women: he speaks[45] of them as being all virtuous in public and, amongst other things, of being economical with their favours in bed. Emilia too jokes with Desdemona about the number of women who "abuse their husbands in such gross kind" in the dark. It all contributes towards what Marilyn French calls Iago's "unremitting hatred of the feminine principle".

But this is not the overriding mood of the whole play. Already we have seen the strength of mind of Desdemona and even in death she refuses to incriminate her husband, as when asked by Emilia who has killed her, she replies: "Nobody, I myself, farewell: / Commend me to my kind lord." And there is Emilia.[46] Once she has grasped the enormity of her husband's complicity in the death of Desdemona, not only does she turn on Othello and refer to him as "ignorant as dirt" and Desdemona's "filthy bargain", her honesty extends to her being outspoken about her husband. Her mistress being murdered, she will not be silent; she refuses to do her duty and obey her husband when he demands she go home. She explains all, totally incriminating her husband for his role in killing "the sweetest innocent that e'er did lift up eye". The sexual jesting is long over: honesty and truth override all other considerations. For this Iago stabs her to death. The point, though, pace Marilyn French, is that it is the two main women in *Othello* who exhibit the life-affirming virtues of love, fidelity, honesty and truthfulness – and perhaps one might add bravery too.

There is one other woman in *Othello*: Bianca, who is best described as a courtesan and a willing sexual partner for Cassio. It is a very small part, necessary for the gulling of Othello, but with her initial exasperation at not having seen Cassio for a week and her final flouncing off she is a realised character, as are Brabantio, the Duke of Venice, Cassio and especially Roderigo. Infatuated with Desdemona, Iago is able to play on Roderigo's hopes and dreams of consummation with her, to use him in his ventures from alerting

---

45   Act 2 Scene 1 l.108–111.
46   One of the daftest pieces of Shakespeare criticism is to be found in Thomas Rymer's *A Short View of Tragedy* (1693), in which he calls Emilia "the meanest woman in the play".

Brabantio to his daughter's elopement, to discrediting Cassio in a drunken brawl and, finally, to try to kill Cassio. Roderigo is simply enjoined to "put money in thy purse" i.e. have enough ready cash to pay Iago for what he affects to be bringing Roderigo towards. He is briefly suspicious of Iago's dealings with him in Act 4 Scene 2 when he points out the cost of jewels he has given Iago to give to Desdemona and that still he has got no further to her bed than his own mind, but the promise of enjoying Desdemona the next night removes the questions from his mind and he commits himself to killing Cassio. He fails in this task and, clearly knowing too much, is then killed by Iago. On one level Roderigo is an example of Iago's powers of manipulation and persuasion, underlining his skills therein and making it easier for us to sympathise with the completely-out-of-his-depths Othello. But in reality too we have a credible portrait of a foolish Venetian gentleman, showing how gullible are those in love. Indeed the individuality of all the characters in *Othello* is one of the great strengths of the play. For me this contrasts greatly with *Timon of Athens*, which, though a later play, has all the signs of being thrown fairly carelessly together, with only Timon and Apemantus possessing individuality and Shakespeare not even being bothered to give some characters names, but calling them simply a poet, a painter, a jeweller and a merchant.

We cannot ignore Iago any longer! The epithet he enjoys, used constantly in juxtaposition to his name, is "honest". Yet he is the man who relishes causing chaos in Othello's mind, leading to the murder of Desdemona; he strings along Roderigo with unrealistic hopes and has to kill him to silence him; he is scornful of women and yet finds himself denounced by his ultimately honest wife, for which denunciation he kills her. Two questions arise: one is what has caused a man with a reputation for honesty to behave so maliciously, and, secondly, does he foresee the consequences when he sets out to get Cassio's place as Othello's lieutenant?

For me this second question is easily answered. No. He tells us in his soliloquy at the end of Act 1 what his aims are: "To get his [Cassio's] place, and to plume up my will." The problem lies with the expression "plume up my will" (which the First Quarto gives as "make up my will"). Whichever word we prefer, I think the meaning is clearly to do with making him feel better about himself and thereby gratifying his ego. In this soliloquy it is established that the trusting Moor can be led by the nose like an ass, and that suggesting that Cassio, the ladies' man, is too familiar with Desdemona will produce the desired replacement of Cassio by himself. By the end of Act 2 Scene 1, though, now on Cyprus, another soliloquy adds to Iago's wish list: he is obsessed with the thought of both Othello and Cassio having had sex with Emilia, and in addition to overthrowing Cassio he now wants to be even with Othello:

> ...wife for wife.
> Or failing so, yet that I put the Moor
> At least into a jealousy so strong
> That judgment cannot cure.

Iago gets nowhere near bedding Desdemona, but – in addition to ensuring his replacing of Cassio – he does fulfil the desire to destroy Othello's judgment and make him mad through jealousy. No other consequences of his actions does Iago foresee, but of course, once the green-eye'd monster is burning within like the mines of sulphur, consequences cannot be foreseen.

Having said that, once Iago's evil magic begins to work, he relishes and revels in it and in the discomfiture he brings to Othello and Cassio. Opportunistically, for example, he uses Desdemona's loss of the mother-precious handkerchief Othello had given her to his own ends and ensures that Othello sees it in Cassio's possession. All along Iago is not sure what he is going to do: he is using situations as they arise. As he himself says: "Knavery's plain face is never seen till used." But it *is* knavery which he is up to. Is it just a free-floating evil in which Iago is indulging or is there motivation for his maliciousness?

Coleridge famously spoke of "motive-hunting of motiveless malignity" with regard to Iago. I actually think he has plenty of motivation. A battle-hardened campaigner – albeit only twenty-eight years of age – he has fought alongside Othello; three "great ones of the city" have spoken in favour of his being given the lieutenantship, but Othello has ignored their advice and given the job to Cassio. Not only is Cassio merely book-learned in the arts of war, he is also one for the ladies – both of which jar with the practical fighting man, cynical in his misogyny. This is motivation enough, I think, for his wanting to cause both distress to Othello for failing to appreciate him, and also for his plotting to usurp Cassio. If we add to this his view of sexual free-for-alls in which he has been cuckolded then there is further motivation for his wanting to destroy Othello and Cassio. The fact that he is a cynic and dismisses love as "merely a lust of the blood and a permission of the will" indicates a nature that has, as it were, given him permission to enjoy Machiavellian scheming which causes so much suffering. His character, his cynical view of the world and his situation all give ample grounds for Iago behaving as he does. And against such a masterly craftsman in the art of undermining and suggestion it is not only Othello who would not be able to handle what is happening to him. As Dante in his *Inferno* writes: "For where the instrument of the mind is joined to evil will and potency, men can make no defence against it."

For me this comment of Dante's is central to our response to Othello. On the surface we have a man so easily manipulated into striking his wife in public and then to suffocating her that, never mind his having done the Venetian state some (very distinguished) service, a response of scorn and horror is demanded from us. Yet, though we do experience horror at his deeds, we do not scorn him; rather we sympathise with this mad, black, murderer. And this is the great human achievement of Shakespeare in *Othello*: a black outsider, a wife-beater and murderer, a man who has lost his honour and reputation too, elicits our sympathies and understanding. Dante explains it: we have seen the evil will and potency of Iago and know that, ultimately – even though Othello does try to stand up against Iago's insinuations and demand "the ocular proof" of Desdemona 's whoredom in Act 3 Scene 3 – he is powerless to withstand the skill of Iago's determined undermining.

There are just three other issues about *Othello* on which I wish to comment before closing. One is what is called the double-time scheme: we witness consecutive action from when the Venetian fleet arrives in Cyprus to the time of Othello's death and that action takes place in thirty-three hours; so, having sailed in separate ships, the question is raised as to *when* Desdemona could have committed adultery with Cassio. But another time scheme is in operation, whereby it is demonstrated that they were all in Cyprus for weeks:

126

Bianca not having seen Cassio for seven days and the arrival of Lodovico from Venice being prime – but not the only – examples of this. It is a part of Shakespeare's genius that the audience/reader is drawn into apparently non-stop action when in reality a number of weeks must have elapsed.

There is also what I called the crisis management skills of the Duke. Faced with the need to send Othello to Cyprus to deal with the Turkish threat and the contradictory demands of Desdemona's father Brabantio that Othello has treacherously seduced his white daughter and should be punished, the Duke in Council listens to Brabantio and Othello and Desdemona and then decisively, with no hedging, accepts what Othello and Desdemona have to say and commits Othello to Cyprus. Listening to all points of view and then making an intelligent, informed decision is a model for all crisis management.

The final point I wish to make is how, as always, order is restored at the end of the play. Shakespeare always questions without being overtly subversive. And the restoration of final order – in this case with the irony of Cassio being appointed Governor of Cyprus – is what Elizabeth and, pertinently, his patron James I, would have wished in times when discontent and disorder were never far from bubbling up to the surface.

In conclusion, to my personal pantheon of favourite Shakespeare plays I wish to add *Othello* to *King Lear* and *Antony and Cleopatra*. All have great characterisations; all have serious, eternally valid themes to explore; all have exquisite poetry; all engage fully. Are there better portraits of insecurity and jealousy than those of Othello, Iago and Roderigo anywhere in literature? *Othello* is a truly great play.

Memorable Quotations From *Othello*

I know my price.
(Iago)

Preferment goes by letter and affection.
(Iago)

Even now, very now, an old black ram
Is tupping your white ewe.
(Iago)

…your daughter and the Moor are now making the beast with two backs.
(Iago)

Keep up your bright swords, for the dew will rust 'em.
(Othello)

Were it my cue to fight, I should have known it,
Without a prompter.
(Othello)

But words are words; I never yet did hear
That the bruis'd heart was pierced through the ear.
(Brabantio)

I saw Othello's visage in his mind.
(Desdemona)

…'tis in our selves that we are thus, or thus: our bodies are gardens, to
the which our wills are gardeners… [love] is merely a lust of the blood and
permissions of the will.
(Iago)

Put money in thy purse.
(Iago)

There are many events in the womb of time, which will be delivered.
(Iago)

I am nothing if not critical.
(Iago)

If it were now to die
'Twere now to be most happy…
(Othello)

Knavery's plain face is never seen, till us'd.
(Iago)

Reputation, reputation, I ha' lost my reputation! I ha' lost the immortal
part, sir, of myself.
(Cassio)

O thereby hangs a tail.
(Clown)

Men should be that they seem.
(Iago)

Good name in man and woman's dear, my lord,
Is the immediate jewel of our souls.
Who steals my purse, steals trash…
(Iago)

O, beware jealousy;
It is the green-ey'd monster, which doth mock
That meat it feeds on.
(Iago)

I know our country disposition well:
In Venice they do let God see the pranks
They dare not show their husbands; their best conscience
Is not to leave undone, but keep unknown…
(Iago)

If I do prove her haggard,
Though that her jesses were my dear heart-strings,
I'd whistle her off, and let her down the wind,
To prey at fortune… O curse of marriage,
That we can call these delicate creatures ours,
And not their appetites.
(Othello)

Dangerous conceits are in their natures poisons
[Which] with a little act upon the blood
Burn like mines of sulphur…
(Iago)

I had been happy if the general camp,
Pioneers, and all, had tasted her sweet body,
So I had nothing known… Farewell, Othello's occupation gone!
(Othello)

'Tis not a year or two shows us a man:
They are all but stomachs, and we all but food;
They eat us hungerly, and when they are full,
They belch us.
(Emilia)

They are not ever jealous for the cause,
But jealous for they are jealous: 'tis a monster,
Begot upon itself, born on itself.
(Emilia)

Had it pleas'd heaven
To try me with affliction, had he rain'd
All kinds of sores and shames on my bare head…
I should have found in some part of my soul
A drop of patience; but, alas, to make me
A fixed figure, for the time of scorn
To point his slow unmoving fingers at…
I here look grim as hell!
(Othello)

…the jewels you have had from me, to deliver to Desdemona, would half
have corrupted a votarist.
(Roderigo)

…who would not make her husband a cuckold to make him a monarch?
(Emilia)

This is the night
That either makes me or undoes me quite.
(Iago)

Put out the light, and then put out the light.
(Othello)

Methinks it should now be a huge eclipse
Of sun and moon, and that the affrighted globe
Should yawn at alteration.
(Othello)

Perchance, Iago, I will ne'er go home.
(Emilia)

O ill-starr'd wench,
Pale as thy smock, when we shall meet at count,
This look of thine will hurl my soul from heaven,
And fiends will snatch at it.
(Othello)

For nought did I in hate, but all in honour.
(Othello)

Demand me nothing, what you know, you know,
From this time forth I never will speak word.
(Iago)

Soft you, a word or two:
I have done then state some service and they know't;
...speak
Of one that lov'd not wisely but too well;
Of one not easily jealous, but being wrought,
Perplex'd in the extreme; of one whose hand,
Like the base Indian, threw a pearl away,
Richer than all his tribe.
(Othello)

CYMBELINE

The premise behind this series of essays on Shakespeare is that we are all better human beings for our involvement with his plays: we understand the machinations, temptations and vicissitudes of the human mind, alongside its capacity to be generous in spirit and to love. Understanding is the beginning of acceptance, tolerance and forgiveness. Unless, perhaps, faced with out-and-out villainy and stupidity, there but for fortune go you and I. *Cymbeline* has a villain, Iachimo, and a stupid man, Cloten, though neither is one hundred per cent reprehensible. It has someone, Imogen, very close to a fairy tale princess, but it is grounded in the realpolitik of Anglo/Roman relationships. As in *Pericles* and *The Winter's Tale* time plays a significant part in development and healing, though in *Cymbeline* we do not witness the significant action which took place some twenty years previous to the onstage drama. Leaving aside the questionably authored *Henry VIII*, it, together with the two above mentioned plays and *The Tempest*, forms a quartet of plays at the end of Shakespeare's writing life which sing the praises of reconciliation and forgiveness.

The history of *Cymbeline* is taken from Holinshed's *Chronicles*, telling of a time when Cymbeline was King of Britain and Augustus was the Roman Emperor. It is a very complex plot, and indeed one of the greatest virtues of this play is the excellence with which Shakespeare controls it and conclusively brings together all the strands. This is the story. Cymbeline had his two sons mysteriously taken away from him some twenty years previously, so his only other child, his daughter Imogen, is in line of succession. Imogen's mother died and Cymbeline has remarried someone simply known as the Queen. The Queen has a son, Cloten, whom she wants to marry Imogen and so increase her already considerable power over the King and the kingdom. Unfortunately Imogen has fallen in love with and married Posthumus (Leonatus), a highly regarded man alongside whom Imogen has been brought up, but who is of lowly birth. On hearing of the marriage a furious Cymbeline banishes Posthumus and Posthumus goes to live in Rome. When in Rome Posthumus is persuaded to enter a bet with Iachimo that he, Iachimo, cannot have sex with Imogen. Craftily, Iachimo is able to give evidence to Posthumus that he did indeed enjoy Imogen's body (though, of course, he didn't) and Posthumus, his faith in womankind shattered, gives orders for Imogen to be killed, but his faithful servant Pisanio is reluctant to carry out the order. Instead he advises Imogen to go to Milford Haven where she will meet the newly arriving Roman ambassador who will give her news of Posthumus.

A good deal happens at Milford Haven before we return to the court. Belarius, a general wrongly banished twenty years previously, is living crudely in Wales, together with Cymbeline's two sons whom he took for revenge and whom he has brought up as his own. Imogen, disguised as a boy Fidele, encounters them and the three siblings form an immediate bond. Cloten too is near Milford Haven, wearing Posthumus' clothes, in which garb he intends to rape Imogen and take her back to court to eventually become his queen. However he offends Cymbeline's elder son Guiderius; they fight, Guiderius kills him and cuts off his head and sends it down river. Imogen discovers the headless body in the clothes of Posthumus, believes Posthumus to be dead and takes a potion to make her sleep which makes her seem dead. Woe all around. As the British have refused to pay tribute to Rome, a Roman army invades and Posthumus and the three wild men from Milford Haven earn honour in the subsequent battle in which the Romans are defeated. Everyone ends up at court where, not without some potentially lethal confusion, all is resolved happily and satisfactorily: Imogen can have her common husband, and her brothers, avid for court life, can assume their rightful places as heirs to the throne. The Queen has conveniently died, revealing her wickedness on her deathbed.

It is quite some story, requiring very careful handling, and I missed out some of the plotting detail. Why, I can hear the reader asking, is Cloten wearing Posthumus' clothes? A good question, to which the answer will be revealed later. In the meantime it must be conceded what a carefully and skilfully crafted play *Cymbeline* is. It is true that some critics have called the plotting clumsy, perhaps based on the midway place transition from the court to Wales – but Shakespeare has a place transition from court to country and a sixteen-year time lapse in *The Winter's Tale*, he has a place transition from Venice to Cyprus in *Othello*, Pericles travels all over the globe and only in *The Tempest*, where significant action has occurred before the play begins, do we find in Shakespeare's late plays a unified sense of time and place. I agree that on one level – the different strands of the story, i.e. the wicked Queen/stepmother, the Roman tribute and invasion, the life in Wales of those who should be courtiers and the Posthumus/ Iachimo wager on Imogen's virtue (this borrowed from the ninth novella of the second day of Boccaccio's *Decameron*) – it would appear that there is almost too much going on, too many apparently diverse strands to the storyline, for a playwright to control. But I think Shakespeare does control all the storylines magnificently and brings them all triumphantly together in the last scenes, where he makes an incontrovertible case for the virtue of forgiveness.

Even Iachimo is forgiven at the end of *Cymbeline*; Iachimo who has cheated in the bet he made with Posthumus, which led to Posthumus' despair and the wished-for death of Imogen. But Iachimo is no Iago.[47] He cheats in order to win a bet and eventually confesses to having done so, whereas by contrast, although Iago's prime motive is to replace Cassio as Othello's lieutenant, he relishes the malevolent letting-rip of the forces that destroy peace of mind and lead to murder. And then Iago is silent, while Iachimo is almost tiresomely loquacious in his confession of his wrongdoing. No, Iachimo is crafty, dishonest, deceitful and living in a moral climate in which young men bedding young women for a bet is seen as an acceptable challenge; but he is not a dyed-in-the-wool villain.

Cymbeline is sometimes regarded as Shakespeare's pantomime, what with an impotent King, a wicked stepmother Queen, two villains (Iachimo and Cloten), a nigh perfect princess and divine intervention (from Jupiter). Pantomimes rely on one-dimensional, recognisable stereotypes. You might argue that that description applies to Cymbeline and it certainly applies to the wicked stepmother Queen, but Iachimo is individualised and, to a certain extent, so is Cloten.

---

47   Interesting that the villains Iago and Iachimo both have the same initial two letters. Think of all the Ians you know…!

What I have in mind is that it is he who articulates the refusal of Cymbeline to pay tribute to the Romans: "Why should we pay tribute? If Caesar can hide the sun from us with a blanket or put the moon in his pocket, we will pay him tribute for light; else, sir, no more tribute." A reasonable and patriotic argument. And then his reason for dressing up in Posthumus' clothes – necessary from the plot's perspective so that Imogen can mistake the headless corpse for that of Posthumus – is explained by the dismissive comment of Imogen's earlier in *Cymbeline* when, rejecting Cloten's protestations of love, she says, speaking of Posthumus:

> *His meanest garment*
> *That ever hath but clipped his body is dearer*
> *In my respect than all the hairs above thee.*

This insult rankles Cloten; hence his persuading Pisario to fetch him his "late master's garments". I would argue that these two incidents are indicative of a man who, despite the aspect of vain and foolish pantomime villainy about him, is individualised into something more than a mere stage villain. In addition they are testament to Shakespeare's careful plotting.

I do not wish to deny that the Queen is monochromatically villainous; nor that Belarius, Guiderius and Arviragus are little more than ciphers, but I do want to look at the characterisations of Posthumus and Imogen and the ideas and values that flow from them.

There is no doubt in anyone's mind, other than that of Cymbeline and his Queen and her son, that by contrast with Cloten who is "too bad for report", Posthumus is a "worthy gentleman", endowed within and without, his like not to be found "thorough the regions of the earth". Orphaned young, he has been brought up alongside Imogen (she calls him "my playfellow"), and there is never a scintilla of a question about their love for each other. That is until Posthumus hears of her apparent seduction by Iachimo. Posthumus entered the bet with Iachimo somewhat reluctantly, but is confident of his success. (Iachimo, incidentally, is pretty confident of success too, in that he is prepared to wager half of his estate on "enjoy[ing] the dearest bodily part of your mistress" and prepared to answer with his sword if he fails.) Posthumus is reluctant to believe Iachimo on his return until Iachimo gives him the final 'proof' - the detail that he has held back until the last: the mole under Imogen's breast. His faith in Imogen destroyed, Posthumus, Othello-like, loses his hitherto irreproachable reputation and vows vengeance on her for her infidelity.

We have seen the effect that women have on men by dint of the power of their sexuality and the consequent mental torture men experience when it is believed that someone else has invaded their fishpond – a torture that leads to destruction in *Othello*. Similarly Posthumus, believing himself betrayed where most he felt secure, gives orders for the death of Imogen and rails against womankind – "We are all bastards" – and blames women for men's vices. Not for Posthumus is the more resigned response of Cymbeline when he hears of his Queen's duplicity: "Who is't can read a woman?" But Posthumus is young and passionately in love. His response to the lost wager and Iachimo declaring Imogen to be 'easy' is to wish he could tear her to pieces and to give orders for her death. An understandable response, perhaps, but forgivable?

Well, he does redeem himself in Act 5 when, believing Imogen dead and his reason for living therefore gone, he lands in Britain with the invading Roman army, determined to fight and die (for such is his wish) for his "lady's kingdom", and together with "a narrow lane, an old man, and two boys" is largely responsible for the British victory. (Rather like Troilus, Posthumus' valour in warfare is predicated on a death wish.) His mental self-flagellation before Cymbeline, admitting responsibility for the supposed death of Imogen, is full of heart-wrenching anguish, and whether we forgive him or not is in fact irrelevant, for Cymbeline and Imogen do – that's what matters. What is more to the point too is that in Posthumus Shakespeare has created a young man, initially a paragon, who falls apart and loses his moral equilibrium when told of his wife's infidelity. It is real characterization: the good, the bad and the ambiguous. Posthumus could not appear in a pantomime.

Can we, though, say the same of Imogen? It is indisputable that, together with Cleopatra, Lady Macbeth, Rosalind and Juliet, she is one of Shakespeare's great female creations. Certain it is that the central action of *Cymbeline* revolves around the relationship between

Imogen and Posthumus, but the question that has to be asked is to what extent she is individuated. The first thing to notice is that her judgment of character is sound: she sees through the Queen's "dissembling courtesy"; there is no way also that she believes or will respond to Cloten's protestations of love; she easily repulses Iachimo's overtures, but then is perhaps too trusting in agreeing to harbour his trunk in her bedchamber, though it is the alleged involvement of Posthumus with the jewels in the trunk which determines that agreement. Imogen clearly possesses a certain courage too as she braves the wilds of Wales disguised as Fidele, though there is a deprecating self-awareness vis-à-vis her courage when she says: "Best draw my sword; and if mine enemy / But fear the sword like me, he'll scarcely look on't."

It is difficult to find fault with Imogen, as indeed it is with Rosalind and Juliet, but she does perhaps lack the energy, the vitality of those two. She does not make things happen: by no stretch of the imagination can she be called passive, but she responds to events which "have a fog in them / That I cannot look through", rather than being herself proactive.[48] Of her love and qualities, though, there is no doubt. Even the gross Cloten confesses that:

> ...she hath all courtly parts more exquisite
> Than lady, ladies, women, from every one
> The best she hath, and she of all compounded
> Outsells them all.

Thus we have a truly exquisite lady, a faithful lover and a pretty shrewd judge of character, blessed with determination and bravery. Not as multi-dimensional as Cleopatra, but far too complex to be a fairy tale princess!

That is all I wish to say about the characterisation. Of course *Cymbeline* has other elements worthy of comment, one of which is certainly non-realistic! I refer to the deus ex machina appearance of Jupiter towards the end of the play, descending as he does in thunder and lightning and on the back of an eagle, to assure us that

---

48   It could be argued that Imogen was proactive before *Cymbeline* began, as Cloten points out that, in marrying Posthumus "you sin against obedience, which you owe your father".

all will be well as "our Jovial star reign'd" at the birth of Posthumus; it is a benevolent star and Jupiter explains the trials of Posthumus with the words: "Whom best I love I cross; to make my gift, / The more delayed, delighted." Arguably this kind of masque[49] grates with modern audiences, but it was a customary feature of plays of the time, and Shakespeare has prepared us for it by there being three references to Jupiter early in *Cymbeline*, i.e. before Posthumus is persuaded of Imogen's infidelity.

Later the Soothsayer refers to "Jove's bird, the Roman eagle", which reinforces the link between Posthumus and Jupiter, as do the numerous references to Posthumus as an eagle. Indeed there is a good deal of bird imagery throughout *Cymbeline*: Cloten is called a "puttock" (a kite, a minor bird of prey), Belarius claims to be perceived as a crow, the Princes in Wales are referred to as "poor, unfledg'd" and most significantly, Iachimo calls Imogen "alone th'Arabian bird" – significantly because this refers to the phoenix which rises from the ashes and Imogen appears too to rise from the dead. This consistent bird imagery adds a depth of texture to the carefully plotted story. I think *Cymbeline* is a significantly well-crafted play.

One of the themes that Shakespeare explores in a number of his plays is that of court versus country life, *As You Like It* and *The Winter's Tale* being prime examples of this. In *Cymbeline* we have the exiled Belarius extolling the virtues of living in rocky caves and seeing the sun, and how much nobler, richer and prouder it makes one feel than does the dishonesty of court life. Guiderius is less enthusiastic, responding to his supposed father's comments with "Happily this life is best / If quiet life be best" and talking of living in "a cell of ignorance", while Arviragus complains, "We have seen nothing." Court life and the opportunities consequent on being Cymbeline's heirs will, at least in the short term, be attractive.

(As an aside it is noteworthy that, alongside John of Gaunt's speech in *Richard II* about this blessed isle [of Britain], we have a similar

---

49   Garrick (who played Posthumus) omitted the masque scene altogether in a mid 18th century production, as did Henry Irving (Iachimo opposite Ellen Terry's Imogen) in a late 19th century production of *Cymbeline*.

paean of praise in *Cymbeline*:

> *The natural bravery of your isle, which stands*
> *As Neptune's park, ribbed and paled in*
> *With rocks unscalable and roaring waters,*
> *With sands that will not bear your enemies' boats*
> *But suck them up to th'topmast.*

Interestingly these words are put into the mouth of the wicked Queen, and with a similar wry humour to that which Shakespeare gives the bestial Caliban in *The Tempest*'s "the isle is full of noises speech", a speech which has come to be seen to refer to Britain, a belief which has been reinforced by its use in the 2012 Olympics opening ceremony.)

There is one other facet of *Cymbeline* totally worthy of comment; I refer to the song *Fear no more the heat o' the sun*. Amongst the many fine songs Shakespeare wrote I regard this as the best. If a song can ever be perfect, this threnody achieves perfection. The couplet "Golden lads and girls all must, / As chimney-sweepers come to dust" has been borrowed or part-borrowed by writers like Housman, T. S. Eliot, Auden and Virginia Woolf – indeed Woolf in *Mrs Dalloway* employs these lines to start her exploration of the death-ridden First World War, and to some extent bind together Mrs Dalloway's internal consciousness. In Samuel Beckett's *Happy Days* "Fear no more the heat o' th'sun" are the lines gone beyond recall that Winnie and her husband are trying to remember. The point is that the song is completely memorable, serious and profound – and haunting. I think it should be simply recited on stage: no music to distract from the words. Perfect song for a funeral – I would welcome it at mine.

That, then, is *Cymbeline*. A well-constructed play with the elements of love, treachery, wagering, international strife, fidelity and loyalty – plus a great song – but above all a play about forgiveness. In the last Act there is the potential for many deaths. Had, for example, the Romans won the battle, most of the Britons at the centre of the play could have died. The Romans lost, but there are still the very real possibilities of Posthumus revenging himself on Iachimo and Cymbeline having Belarius killed. The defeated Romans too could have been slaughtered. None of this happens. Posthumus sets the tone by forgiving Iachimo and Cymbeline follows: "Pardon's the word to all." Cymbeline even agrees to pay tribute to Rome, bringing the Roman eagle and the protection Posthumus received from Jupiter together too. All is harmony.

Ultimately forgiveness and harmony are the essence of *Cymbeline*. The play has been carefully plotted to lead to this conclusion. This is the mature Shakespeare expressing what one critic[50] has called "a vision of perfect tranquillity". For me the human values embedded deeply in forgiveness and striving to live together in harmony can never be overstated. *Cymbeline* is an outstanding dramatic presentation of these values.

---

50   J. M Nosworthy in his introduction to the Arden edition of *Cymbeline*.

Memorable Quotations From *Cymbeline*

Boldness be my friend.
(Iachimo)

...doubting things go ill often hurts more
Than to be sure they do.
(Imogen)

When a gentleman is disposed to swear, it is not for any standers-by to curtail his oaths.
(Cloten)

Winning will put any man into courage.
(Cloten)

Our countrymen
Are men more ordered than when Julius Caesar
Smiled at their lack of skill but found their courage
Worthy his frowning at.
(Posthumus)

We are all bastards,
...Some coiner with his tools
Made me a counterfeit... there's no motion
That tends to vice in man but I affirm
It is the woman's part...
For even to vice
They are not constant.
(Posthumus)

The natural bravery of your isle, which stands
As Neptune's park, ribbed and paled in
With rocks unscalable and roaring waters,
With sands that will not bear your enemies' boats
But suck them up to th' topmast.
(Queen)

Why should we pay tribute? If Caesar can hide the sun from us with a
blanket or put the moon in his pocket, we will pay him tribute for light; else,
sir, no more tribute.
(Cloten)

O for a horse with wings!
(Imogen)

O, this life
Is nobler than attending for a check,
Richer than doing nothing for a bribe,
Prouder than rustling in unpaid-for silk.
(Belarius)

What shall I need to draw my sword? The paper
Hath cut her throat already. No, 'tis slander,
Whose edge is sharper than the sword, whose tongue
Outvenoms all the worms of Nile, whose breath
Rides on the posting winds and doth belie
All corners of the world.
(Pisanio)

I have not slept one wink.
(Pisanio)

Hath Britain all the sun that shines?
(Imogen)

I see a man's life is a tedious one.
(Imogen)

And falsehood is worse in kings than beggars.
(Imogen)

Cowards father cowards and base things sire base.
(Belarius)

Thersites' body is as good as Ajax
When neither are alive.
(Guiderius)

Fear no more the heat o' th' sun
Nor the furious winter's rages;
Thou thy wordly task hast done,
Home art gone and ta'en thy wages.
Golden lads and girls all must,
As chimney-sweepers, come to dust.
Fear no more the frown o' th' great;
Thou art past the tyrant's stroke...
The scepter, learning, physic, must
All follow this and come to dust...
All lovers young, all lovers must
Consign to thee and come to dust...
(Guiderius and Arviragus)

Whom best I love I cross; to make my gift,
The more delayed, delighted.
(Jupiter)

...he that sleeps feels not the tooth-ache.
(Jailer)

Who is't can read a woman?
(Cymbeline)

Does the world go round?
(Cymbeline)

144

The pow'r that I have on you is to spare you;
The malice towards you to forgive you. Live,
And deal with others better.
(Posthumus)

Pardon's the word to all.
(Cymbeline)

THE TEMPEST

After *Cymbeline* the obvious play to consider is *The Tempest*, mainly because it again pursues the themes of reconciliation and forgiveness but with a deal more soul-searching, as the possibility of retribution, motivated by anger, is presented as a very real alternative: forgiveness or revenge is the question. There are other major themes running through the play too: the perennial discussion of nature as opposed to nurture and the contrast between nature and art; the corruption associated with power; the possible identification of Shakespeare with Prospero, as he too bids adieu to his art. *The Tempest* is really Shakespeare's last word[51] on his ongoing exploration in his plays of what it is to be human and what are the abiding values therein.

The Tempest and *Love's Labours Lost* are the only Shakespeare plays whose plots are not taken, to a greater or lesser degree, from another literary source. There was, however, a significant contemporary story which almost certainly fuelled Shakespeare's imagination. In June 1609 a fleet of nine ships had set off from Plymouth, carrying would-be Virginia colonists. A storm off the Bermudas on the 20th July had separated the ships, eight of which eventually, in a degree of disarray, made it to Jamestown, but the other ship, the flagship the *Sea-Venture*, was not seen again and therefore deemed lost. Indeed, the ship itself was lost, but in May of the following year the occupants of the *Sea-Venture* arrived in Jamestown in two small self-built ships. They had been shipwrecked in the Bermudas on what was known as the Isle of Devils, but which had in fact proved advantageous to life, being almost an island paradise. News of this apparent miracle reached London in September 1610. *The Tempest* was written in 1611, and although the shipwreck that prefaces the

51   I *do* see *The Tempest* as Shakespeare's last play. I accept that he wrote some scenes in *Henry VIII* but it was perhaps a reluctant contribution/collaboration.

story that unfolds in *The Tempest* takes place on the return voyage from Tunis to Naples – and thus nowhere near the Bermudas – the story I am about to tell is clearly and strongly influenced by this 'miracle' in the Bermudas.

The Tempest begins with a number of people being shipwrecked on an island, in a tempest which we are soon informed was caused by the art and magic of the ruler of the island, Prospero. Prospero explains to his daughter, Miranda, why he has caused the storm: once upon a time he was ruler of Milan, but in order to study his books he deputed his power to his brother Antonio, who then seized power and put Prospero and Miranda into a scarcely seaworthy vessel and left them at sea. Providence had brought them to the island and now Fortune, some twelve years later, has brought together Antonio and his confederate in the overthrow of Prospero: Alonso, King of Naples, and Alonso's brother Sebastian – all returning home from Tunis (where Alonso's daughter, Claribel, has been married to the King of Carthage) and all enemies of Prospero. They are all now in Prospero's power, exacted largely by his sprite Ariel who at one moment prevents Alonso from being murdered by his brother so that he too can usurp him and become King of Naples. An honest old councillor, Gonzalo, is with them too and narrowly escapes murder. Prospero has his enemies in his power: will he revenge or forgive?

The ship's crew has largely been left to sleep aboard the ship safely in harbour, but three others are thrown onto the island: Stephano, the ship's butler, and Trinculo the jester are two of them. They form an alcohol-fuelled alliance with Caliban, "a savage and deformed slave" who had exclusive possession of the island until the arrival of Prospero and Miranda, and they are used by Shakespeare partly for comic effect, but also form a subplot as they wish to take over rulership of the island by rape and murder.

Then there is Ferdinand, son of the King of Naples, who mutually falls in love with Miranda as Prospero desired, though he does control the speed of their courtship. So what will happen? We know it is a fruitful and prosperous island. What will Prospero do now he has his enemies in his power? What will happen to Stephano and Trinculo and Caliban? Will Ariel be given the freedom he is demanding? Will Ferdinand and Miranda marry and thus give promise of a reconciled future? And what of Prospero himself and his magic powers, evidenced by his ability to conjure spirits and present masques and banquets: will he return to the real world, forswearing his magic? Yes is the answer to that last question, but it is not an enthusiastic, triumphant return. And yes, he does proclaim "The rarer action is in virtue than in vengeance", apparently taking his lead from Ariel, but there may not be such a blanket forgiveness and reconciliation as there is in *Cymbeline*. It is an intriguing play.

But it is a play that is far from flawless. The comic scenes between Stephano, Trinculo and Caliban are pretty clunkily unfunny. Verbal felicities are not forthcoming and there is some rather laboured humour, principally based on confusion and the drinking of alcohol. Broad slapstick is the only way to play it; I feel it would have been more appreciated by the audience of Shakespeare's day than it is today. Having said that, it is a necessary element of the plot as it provides a parallel commentary on the lure of power and rulership, together with the lengths to which people will go to obtain such power.

Another weakness of *The Tempest* is, for me, the lengthy exposition in Act 1 Scene 2 wherein Prospero tells Miranda the backdrop to the events that are about to unfold on the island. The play opens with a dramatic storm and then it all goes flat, as there is neither action nor character development while Prospero explains to his daughter their history for one hundred and eighty-six lines, eventually sending Miranda to sleep. Shakespeare the dramatist is, though, very aware of the potential boredom of such an exposition, and, seeing her attention flagging, he challenges Miranda's (our?) alertness with five interjections to the narrative such as "I pray thee mark me", "Dost thou attend me?" and "Dost thou hear?" The modern-day audience with its increasingly limited attention span might well be restless by line 187, but thanks to those interjections, will probably have heard Prospero out.

Before I consider the really serious issues of *The Tempest* there are one or two other discussion points to consider. I mentioned there being no character development in Act 1 Scene 2, but it has been argued that there is no character development anywhere in the play – intentionally so, as Shakespeare is manipulating his characters to the desired conclusion so that they represent nothing more than symbols: Prospero representing wisdom, Antonio wickedness, Caliban bestiality, Miranda purity and so on. It is a view with which I partly concur. We know Shakespeare can create complex characters who gain wisdom through suffering – Lear and Othello being the prime examples of this – but in *The Tempest* this is not Shakespeare's focus. All the human characters are being manipulated by Shakespeare towards a determined resolution, in much the same way as Prospero is manipulating the events on the island through his "most potent art". In many ways *The Tempest* is more obviously a construct than any other Shakespeare play in so far as, once on the island, non-human events dominate, from the various magical and musical interventions of Ariel to the banquet presented by spirits to Stephano and his troupe and suddenly withdrawn, and in the midst of all this is the stylised wedding masque with Juno and Ceres. It is all so (deliberately) artful! (Yet the masque does echo the human theme of Ferdinand's not breaking Miranda's "virgin knot" before the marriage ceremony.) One critic – Enid Welsford in *The Court Masque* (1927) – has even argued that *The Tempest* is in fact a dramatised masque. There is, I feel, more than a grain of truth in this, and it is perhaps this which causes some contemporary theatregoers, used to the presentation and working-out of issues within a realistic setting, to baulk at *The Tempest*. Having said that, and acknowledged the artificiality of the play with humans being manipulated like pawns by Prospero, things are, as ever with Shakespeare, not that simple: most conflict takes place within the non-humans Ariel and Caliban, and the central issue of the play is the conflicted Prospero, vis-à-vis what he will do with his enemies now he has them at his mercy. All important matters, to which I will return.

First, though, we must discuss the nature/nurture issue raised in *The Tempest*. As the somewhat idealistic, utopian Gonzalo – he envisages a society with no need for magistrates, no weapons, no riches and no poverty, with everyone innocent and idle – points out: "Here is everything advantageous to life." The growth is lush and green. Nature flourishes, but when it comes to human nature we are presented with the two polarities of Miranda and Caliban, with all the other characters occupying different places on the continuum. By nature Miranda is innocent and Caliban is bestial, yet both have been taught by the same would-be nurturer, Prospero. What this demonstrates is that even the best teaching in the world cannot fundamentally affect someone's nature. One would like to think that someone with an awareness of words and literature would thereby be enabled to develop a sensitive tolerance, but Caliban gives the lie to this: "You taught me language, and my profit on't / Is, I know how to curse."

Maybe Miranda was driven from the court before it had begun to exercise its corrupting influence on her, whereas Caliban was under the influence of his dam Sycorax in the early years of his life. Maybe. The nurture/nature discussion continues to rage in 2013 as it did in 1611. Prospero is clear, though, about what he thinks of Caliban:

> *A devil, a born devil, on whose nature*
> *Nurture can never stick; on whom my pains,*
> *Humanely taken, all, all lost, quite lost!*

A brief word about Gonzalo: he does see things differently and he is a fascinating minor character. Utopian in words and blind to the fogs and diseases of the island, he it was who enabled Prospero and Miranda to survive their expulsion from Milan. Whereas the courts of Naples and Milan would appear to be corrupt – witness Antonio and Sebastian particularly – Gonzalo is the exception to any generalisation we might wish to make. As with the nature/nurture debate Shakespeare, as in everything he writes, is never dogmatic. Court life, with its intrigues of "who's in, who's out" (Lear) is likely to breed corruption, but not necessarily.

Order, though, is important to Shakespeare. As we have seen, there is always a restoration of a measure of order, however uncertain we the audience may feel about it, at the end of each play. If order and respect for order break down, as Ulysses in *Troilus and Cressida* points out, we have a recipe for chaos. Shakespeare adheres to this thinking and I think it requires an unwarranted degree of cynicism to believe that he does so, and therefore accepts hierarchies, merely to appease his royal patrons. There is a natural order which various actions in *The Tempest* attempt to subvert: Prospero initially abdicated his responsibilities by handing over the temporary governorship of Milan to Antonio; Sebastian is tempted – and without the intervention of Ariel, would have succeeded – to kill his father the king; and

Caliban, an obviously inferior breed, preposterously thinks he can overthrow Prospero. It can even be argued that Prospero erred in extending to Caliban the gift of language for he is an inferior creature and language is fit only for humans – to each his place in the order of things!

Moving from the order of things to the nature of things. It must be remembered that, though Caliban may be bestial, he is not a beast, and though Ariel is a fairy sprite, he is not an abstract entity: both have human feelings. Caliban does not simply represent crude, unrestructured nature, just as Prospero is not merely an example of a magician living a cerebral life, interested only in his art. Human aspirations – rulership, freedom, revenge, forgiveness – dominate the themes of *The Tempest*, and just as human nature is shown in all its complexities, so is the island. On one hand it is an isle of wonder but we also learn from Trinculo that there is "neither bush nor shrub" to shelter in and protect from an impending storm: Gonzalo's encomium about the island is only a partial truth. Prospero's agent Ariel leads Trinculo, Stephano and Caliban to the filthy pool from which they emerge smelling of horse piss, but this pool is a natural feature of the island and so are the "toothed briers, sharp furzes, pricking goss[52], and thorns" through which they are led. Nature in all its forms.

Prospero's magic takes many forms too. A celebratory nuptial masque is one thing, but he does use it for punitive purposes against Caliban too. It is open to misuse. We do not have to go so far as to agree with Caliban that without the power of his books Prospero is but a sot, though we do know that without his art Prospero will experience a greatly significant diminution of his power. But one cannot live by art alone. Always when Prospero has been exercising his art the motivation has been a human one. (Human) nature is at the heart of all things, so Prospero inevitably has to bow to this truth and relinquish his "rough magic". By doing so he is choosing the path to death, where "every third thought shall be my grave". The process of relinquishing acquired skills as one inevitably moves towards death is a natural one. Prospero faces up to this. Art can transform and illuminate, but nature, whether it be wild in tooth and claw or benign, or (as it most frequently is) somewhere in between,

---

52   goss = gorse.

is inescapable.

Humans have to make moral decisions. It is one thing to have, by his art, ensured that all his enemies are in his power; it is something else to decide what course of action he then will have to take. Prospero is faced with a dilemma, which is a human dilemma. We know that – with some justification, for rape and murder were on his agenda – Caliban has been punished and tormented by Prospero, but we also know that he has a temper, for when, early in the play, Ariel reminds him of his promise to free him, Prospero rounds on him, calling him a "malignant thing". And Prospero has every reason to be revenged on Antonio and Alonso, and especially Antonio who shipped him and Miranda out to sea, expecting their deaths by drowning. Yet he eventually chooses to forgive. Why? Is it just that he is moved to do so by the words of Ariel – that were he human, he would feel tender towards his captives – and these words suddenly determine Prospero's course of action; that he will use his "nobler reason" rather than his "fury"? Well, yes and no! Clearly, having made the initial use of "bountiful Fortune" bringing his enemies close by the island and knowing that his future fortunes depend on his responding to the current auspicious star, Prospero's mind has been working for some time on what to do with his enemies. Forgiveness has always been a possibility but Ariel's comment triggers an immediate, human response. Knowing the later plays of Shakespeare, there was never going to be any other response.

This reconciliation and forgiveness is not a sentimental one: Prospero calls Antonio and Sebastian unnatural and speaks of his brother as wicked and "whom to call brother would even infect my mouth"; yet he forgives all his rankest faults. Twelve years of anger cannot vanish overnight. And there is no pretence about Antonio and Sebastian being anything other than unpleasant people, as they jest about the appearance and marketability of Stephano, Trinculo and Caliban. Prospero is much more gentle with Alonso, who is mourning the apparent loss of his son, and he is, of course, genuinely delighted to see Gonzalo. Ariel is freed, but Caliban has to earn his forgiveness by trimming Prospero's cell handsomely.

So the forgiveness is more a calculated and cerebral one than appears at the end of *Cymbeline* and, as such, is more realistic. It is the union of Naples and Milan, symbolised by the love of Ferdinand and Miranda, which is most important. The union has been anticipated by Prospero, and Ferdinand as a patient log-bearer has had to show restraint and earn Miranda. But once Ferdinand has proved himself worthy of his daughter, Prospero provides them with the blessings of the goddesses Iris, Juno and Ceres to celebrate their contract of true love – a contract, blessed by Alonso too, on which future peace and stability will be based. That is the true harmony at the end of *The Tempest*.

So is it appropriate to identify Shakespeare the playwright with Prospero the magician? There are three valedictory speeches from Prospero as he puts aside his art. There is the conventional epilogue beginning "Now my charms are all o'erthrown", but more significant are the other two (magnificent) speeches. In the "ye elves of hills..." speech Prospero reminisces about having "bedimmed the noontide sun", created thunderbolts and opened graves, enabling the dead to live. These powers he attributes to his "so potent art". One more spell[53] and he will break his magic staff and bury his magic book in the depths of the ocean. Is this Shakespeare saying farewell to his art too? The parallels are there. And when earlier, in Act 4 Scene 1, Prospero speaks of "our revels now are ended" he makes his point with references to actors and "the great globe itself". There is modesty in his saying that not even a "rack"[54] will be left behind, but he is talking of coming to the end of life. The words and wisdom – and control – of Prospero dominate *The Tempest* as have those of Shakespeare throughout his working life. Prospero and Shakespeare are clearly not identical, but the parallels are obvious. Both have come to the end of their creative life and are saying goodbye to their art; both are acknowledging the power of nature as they move towards death. In this last play Shakespeare creates a magic island where real power struggles take place, where the issue of whether it is best to forgive or pursue vengeance is finally worked out and where harmony and hope are promised through the next generation. One almost forgets the music and poetry too! It is a hell of a play to go out on...

---

53   This refers to his immediate plans for his captives on the island. I don't think that by any stretch of the imagination it can refer to *Henry VIII*.

54   A light trace of cloud.

Memorable Quotations From *The Tempest*

What care these roarers for the name of king?
(Boatswain)

There's no harm done.
(Prospero)

What sees thou else
In the dark backward and abysm of time?
(Prospero)

My library
Was dukedom large enough.
(Prospero)

Is there more toil?
(Ariel)

You taught me language, and my profit on't
Is, I know how to curse.
(Caliban)

Come unto these yellow sands,
And then take hands.
(Ariel)

This music crept by me upon the waters.
(Ferdinand)

Full fathom five thy father lies;
Of his bones are coral made
Those are pearls that were his eyes;
Nothing of him that doth fade
But doth suffer a sea change.
(Ariel)

At the first sight
They have changed eyes.
(Prospero)

...too light winning makes the prize light.
(Prospero)

There's nothing ill can dwell in such a temple.
(Miranda)

He receives comfort like cold porridge.
(Sebastian)

Here is everything advantageous to life.
(Gonzalo)

What have we here? A man or a fish?... in England... when they will
not give a doit to relieve a lame beggar, they will lay out ten to see a dead
Indian.
(Trinculo)

Misery acquaints a man with strange bedfellows.
(Trinculo)

But none of us cared for Kate.
(Stephano)

There be some sports are painful, and their labour
Delight in them sets off.
(Ferdinand)

...for your sake
Am I this patient log-man.
(Ferdinand)

Be not afeard: this isle is full of noises,
Sounds and sweet airs that give delight and hurt not...
(Caliban)

My high charms work... They now are in my power.
(Prospero)

Do not give dalliance
Too much the rein: the strongest oaths are straw
To th' fire i' th' blood.
(Prospero)

So rare a wond'red father and a wise
Makes this place Paradise.
(Ferdinand)

Our revels now are ended. These our actors...
Are melted into air, into thin air;
...We are such stuff
As dreams are made on, and our little life
Is rounded with a sleep.
(Prospero)

A devil, a born devil, on whose nature
Nurture can never stick.
(Prospero)

Now does my project gather to a head.
(Prospero)

Your charm so strongly works 'em,
That if you now beheld them, your affections
Would become tender.
(Ariel)
Dost thou think so, spirit?
(Prospero)

Mine would, sir, were I human.
(Ariel)

Yet with my nobler reason 'gainst my fury
Do I take part. The rarer action is
In virtue than in vengeance.
(Prospero)

But this rough magic
I here abjure; and when I have required
Some heavenly music… I'll break my staff,
Bury it certain fathoms in the earth,
And deeper than did ever plummet sound
I'll drown my book.
(Prospero)

O, wonder!
How many godly creatures are there here!
How beauteous mankind is! O brave new world
That has such people in't!
(Miranda)

Two of these fellows you
Must know and own; this thing of darkness I
Acknowledge mine.
(Prospero)

Every third thought shall be my grave.
(Prospero)

Now my charms are all o'erthrown…
As you from crimes would pardoned be,
Let your indulgence set me free.
(Prospero)

ALL'S WELL THAT ENDS WELL

With such a title it would appear that this is the obvious play with which to continue the pursuit of plays with happy endings. But horses must be held. Maybe Shakespeare has titled the play with his tongue in his cheek: there are, after all, more 'if's in *All's Well That Ends Well* than in any other of his plays, and the play, as we shall see, does not end with an unconditional certainty. In a moment I will tell the story of the play, but before then, just a little background.

First of all, there is no evidence of the play having been performed in Shakespeare's lifetime – indeed the earliest performance of the play would seem to have been in 1741, and from that performance it gained the reputation, along with *Macbeth*, for being an unlucky play, as the first night had to be delayed because of illness in the actor playing the King, and when the first night did take place, and subsequently, various actors became ill. Some would say that this is why it is infrequently performed: others – including me – would say that the reason for its lack of popularity is because it is not a very good play. When you have a play that the critics find unsatisfactory the name Middleton is often trotted out as being a likely co-author. I am not convinced of this, though there is a good deal of prose and easy rhyming couplets in the text which indicate a play that has been perhaps carelessly tossed off.

The dating of the play – 1604–1605 – does somewhat perplex me. I accept that internal evidence would make this the most likely time of writing, but then we find *All's Well That Ends Well*, together with *Timon of Athens*, wedged between the wonderful plays *Othello* and *King Lear*, and these two latter plays are followed by seven plays of undoubted quality. Clearly I am not in love with *All's Well That Ends Well* (nor do I feel much affection for *Timon of Athens*). It is all very well to call it – along with *Measure for Measure, Troilus and Cressida*

159

and *Hamlet* – a 'problem play', but *Measure for Measure* gives us a discussion on governance and relative morality, *Troilus and Cressida* provides an exploration of sexual morality and order, and *Hamlet* is a profound psychological study. I can see nothing of merit along any of these lines in *All's Well That Ends Well*. Perhaps as I tell the story and discuss the characters and the main issues the play will yield more…

At the centre of the plot of *All's Well That Ends Well* are the two young people, Bertram and Helena. Both have lost their fathers, but whereas Bertram's father was the Count of Rossillion, Helena's was of more ordinary origins: the doctor, Gerard de Narbon. Helena is under the wardship of Bertram's mother, the Countess of Rossillion, and has fallen desperately in love with Bertram. Bertram regards Helena as inferior and will have nothing to do with her; he is a young man who wants to bed as many virgins as possible. However, the French king is dying and none of his doctors can save him. Helena, having acquired some skills from her father, is eventually allowed to try to cure the King. She succeeds! For payment she asks to be permitted to choose any young man for a husband. She, of course, chooses Bertram. He is horrified and initially refuses to marry, but, fearing the wrath of the King, goes through with the wedding ceremony – and immediately runs off to display a certain amount of valour in the internal wars in Italy. The marriage is not consummated; indeed Bertram vows that he and Helena will never live together as man and wife until she gets the family ring from off his finger and becomes pregnant by him – apparently impossible conditions. However (!) Helena, fearing that she has sent Bertram to possible death in Italy, leaves France, thus enabling him to return home at some future time, while she sets off on a pilgrimage to Saint Jacques le Grand at Compestella in North West Spain. En route she comes across a young woman, Diana, whom Bertram is trying to bed: she persuades Diana to agree to Bertram's wooing in exchange for the family ring and then substitutes herself for Diana in bed. Hence she obtains the ring and also becomes pregnant. Everyone then, including the King, returns to Rossillion; Bertram resorts to lies and slander to extricate himself from the situation, but eventually capitulates and agrees to live with Helena as man and wife. And thus all's well that ends well…

That's the essence of the story. I will discuss some of the other (mainly older) characters and the comedy and also the moral touchstone character, Parolles, in a moment, but perhaps so far the bed-substitution trick will have been recognised from *Measure for Measure*, as will the equally well-used obtaining-the-ring trick from *The Merchant of Venice*. *All's Well That Ends Well* begins to feel like a quickly-thrown-together potboiler. Just as Graham Greene separated some of his lesser novels from such masterpieces as *The Heart of the Matter*, *The Power and the Glory*, *The Comedians* and *A Burnt-Out Case* by calling them "entertainments", so it could well be appropriate to similarly label *All's Well That Ends Well* and *Timon of Athens*.

When we consider the older characters in *All's Well That Ends Well*, they come across much more sympathetically than do the younger ones.[55] The part of the Countess of Rossillion is described by Shaw as "the most beautiful old woman's part ever written"; she is a good woman who can see the sounder moral standards her ward possesses in contrast to her son, whom she rejects. Wise and compassionate, I have seen her played by Peggy Ashcroft and, in more recent years, by Judi Dench, and also by Celia Johnson in the *BBC Television Shakespeare* series in the 1980s. It really is a splendidly sympathetic role but, at the fringes of the action, cannot carry the play. Lafew, described simply as an old Lord, is also sympathetic, dispensing occasional wisdom and seeing through both Parolles and Bertram into the callousness of their souls. The King too appears to have no villainy in him: he does not see virtue as a prerogative only of the wealthy, and it is perfectly reasonable for a king to wish his decrees to be carried out; moreover he is also prepared to reward and forgive – the latter perhaps too easily, as we shall see. Even the old dead, like Helena's father, are spoken well of, and Bertram's father is especially praised: the King, unbidden, acknowledges the medical skills of Gerard de Narbon and eulogises the friendship and humility of Bertram's father. Shakespeare portrays the old generously in *All's Well That Ends Well*.

Everything, however, about his portrayal of Helena and Bertram is much more contentious. Before we look at that, though, a few words about Parolles. Arguably he is the most interesting character in the

---

55   There are, in fact, two young French lords who are not dreadful exemplars of youth.

play; a kind of sub-Falstaff figure in that he is the friend, adviser and confidant of the young Bertram, as was Falstaff to the young Prince Hal. Like Falstaff he is a coward and a liar, but he lacks Falstaff's chutzpah and presence, attributes which are necessary for the audience to warm to him. Parolles, though, is not merely the butt of much of the laughter in *All's Well That Ends Well* (as he is when, for example, he is blindfolded and, believing himself to have been captured by the enemy, he calls Bertram "a foolish, idle boy", is even more dismissive of two of his captors and gives away, from fear and not from torture, military secrets); he is also the source of much laughter as he jousts verbally with Lafew and Helena. With Helena it is about her virginity, in the course of which he makes the admirable (it seems to me) point that virginity is "made of self-love" and that to extol the virtues of virginity is to rubbish your mother and be disobedient. Be that as it may, the most significant aspect of the quite lengthy 'virginity' exchange is that it shows not only the feisty spirit of Helena but also her ripeness – she is sexually ready, but only for Bertram. Helena actually gives us the essence of Parolles' character when he first enters and she labels him "a notorious liar... a great way fool, solely a coward". But Parolles does possess a certain energy. The play benefits from his presence and although he is totally discredited by the end of *All's Well That Ends Well*, we are confident – as he is too – of his survival and are pleased when Lafew extends hospitality to him, albeit the kind of hospitality you extend to a beggar: "Though you are a fool and a knave, you shall eat."

Time to look at Helena. Desperately in love with Bertram – simply because of his good looks, it would seem – and aware that her suit is "presumptuous" and that "I love in vain, strive against hope", she uses the opportunity afforded her by the King's illness to follow Bertram to court where, having cured the King, she obliges him to fulfil his part of the deal: that she can choose whom to marry. She chooses Bertram, to his expressed horror; which is when he runs away from her to the Italian wars. Fearing that he might be killed in war, and also knowing that her presence in France prevents him from returning home, Helena goes away on a pilgrimage, expressly to allow Bertram to come home to safety. All actions motivated by love, as is her deceitful bedding of him, and by the end of the play she has her man! So have we not here a strong, determined woman, prepared to risk her life for love (had she not cured the King, her life was forfeit) and praised by the King for her "youth, beauty, wisdom, courage"? What is there to dislike about her? Shaw likened Helena to Nora in Ibsen's *A Doll's House* as a New Woman figure. A feminist precursor?

Yet, yet, yet... She is obsessive about Bertram, almost as though she is playing at being in love[56]: he gives her a goal and a purpose and a reason to behave nobly and apparently self-sacrificingly at times. But there is absolutely no consideration for Bertram! It is as though he is a quarry to be hunted down and killed (or inescapably married). One can commend Helena's resolution and her skilful opportunism vis-à-vis swapping places with Diana in bed, but she has no glimmer of understanding of Bertram's feelings. Her pursuit is an obsessive pursuit, rather like that of a stalker, which would be fine if she were big game hunting but her target is Bertram and despicable as he is, he is human! Helena is prepared to sacrifice herself and do what it takes to corner and marry a mere man. New Woman and/or feminist? Are you having a laugh?

In truth, Bertram *is* despicable. He scorns Helena largely on account of her social inferiority. He prefers the company of Parolles to that of Helena. He gives the valued family ring to (as he thought) Diana and, having bedded her, never expects to see her again. He then tries to lie and slander his way out of the weight of evidence against him when his perfidy is revealed to all. He does eventually and suddenly capitulate to the King and Helena, though this is pretty much forced upon him. The only good thing that can be said about him is that he gave honourable service in the Italian wars. Evaluated on any moral scale, as distinct from social scale, he comes well below Helena. There is almost nothing likeable about him, which is Shakespeare's intention. The storyline is taken from Boccacio's *De Cameron* and, in the words of Kenneth Muir[57]: "it is worth remembering that all Bertram's worst traits were added by Shakespeare – his friendship with Parolles, his rejoicing at the death of his wife[58], his promise of marriage to the girl in Florence, the parting with the ancestral

56   See my similar comments about Orsino and Olivia in the essay on *Twelfth Night*.
57   In *Shakespeare's Comic Sequence*, Liverpool 1979.
58   Helena's death is a supposed one, accepted by all.

heirloom, his smirching of the girl's character".

What had Shakespeare in mind? We have an obsessive, selfish heroine; we have a callow, lying hero. Our sympathies are enlisted for neither of them. Perhaps the ending will be magical, as in *The Winter's Tale*, and/or pulled skilfully together as in *Cymbeline*, but even when we pass over the lack of self-awareness of Helena and Bertram in comparison with the characters in those two plays, there remains no redemption in the conclusion of *All's Well That Ends Well*.

In fact the ending is rushed. There is scarcely a hundred lines between the unexpected entrance of the (obviously alive) Helena[59] and everything being neatly wrapped up – Bertram accepting Helena and the King offering Diana a dower and a choice of husband. But do Bertram and Helena accept each other? There is an 'if' in Bertram's yielding and a threat in Helena's conditional acceptance, and there is no indication that either has changed and that mutual love (as distinct from obsession and repulsion) can bond them together: they are no Beatrice and Benedict. It is easy to accept the argument that Shakespeare titled *All's Well That Ends Well* with his tongue firmly in his cheek.

Even the Epilogue, spoken by the King, is a brief one. It really does feel as though Shakespeare is in a hurry to finish the play. The King is in a mood of complete forgiveness: he has "forgiven and forgotten" all Bertram's transgressions: "we are reconciled". He wants to toll "sweet Helen's knell, and now forget her". There is a kind of bland complacency in the last Act. No soul-searching, no reflection, no agony – nothing like Prospero. Yes, there is the familiar forgiveness and reconciliation at the end, but it is imposed and not worked through. There is just a glib hastening towards a shallow resolution.

I am not alone in finding it difficult to take to *All's Well That Ends Well*: in his introduction to the Arden edition of the play Osborne Brigstock writes: "everyone who reads this play is at first shocked

---

59   There is no magic in Helena's apparent restoration to life as there is with Hermione in *The Winter's Tale*. She makes an ordinary entrance.

and perplexed by the revolting idea that underlies the plot" and, writing of a 1953 Stratford production of the play, the theatre critic T. C. Worsley wrote: "What a ridiculous, badly-written, ill-constructed play *All's Well That Ends Well* is!... Only piety keeps it in the repertoire, and that piety is surely misplaced... No audience of sensible people would solemnly tolerate such rubbish."

I do not wish to voice my criticisms of the play quite so stridently, but I do concur with the opinion that this is one of Shakespeare's worst plays. If there is a revered actress playing the Countess or a splendid comic actor playing Parolles I would recommend seeing the play, but do not expect to be moved and do expect to be dissatisfied. Jeremy Hardy, quite recently on the radio, opined that Shakespeare's tragedies were brilliant plays but that the rest of his output was pretty rubbishy. He was right about the tragedies being the height of Shakespeare's achievement but wrong about the blanket condemnation of all the other plays. But if Jeremy Hardy had *All's Well That Ends Well* in the forefront of his mind, I can at least understand where he is coming from...

Memorable Quotations From *All's Well That Ends Well*

Moderate lamentation is the right of the dead, excessive grief the enemy to the living.
(Lafew)

The hind that would be mated by the lion
Must die for love.
(Helena)

To speak on the part of virginity is to accuse your mothers, which is most infallible disobedience... Besides, virginity is peevish, proud, idle, made of self-love which is the most inhibited sin in the canon... 'tis a withered pear.
(Parolles)

"Let me not live," quoth he,
"After my flame lacks oil, to be the snuff
Of younger spirits..."
(King)

Those girls of Italy, take heed of them:
They say our French lack language to deny
If they demand. Beware of being captives
Before you serve.
(King)

They say miracles are past, and we have our philosophical persons to make modern and familiar, things supernatural and causeless. Hence is it that we make trifles of terrors, ensconcing ourselves into seeming knowledge when we should submit ourselves to an unknown fear.
(Lafew)

A young man married is a man that's marred.
(Parolles)

I am a simple maid, and therein wealthiest.
(Helena)

Wars is no strife
To the dark house and the detested wife.
(Bertram)

The soul of this man is his clothes. Trust him not in matter of heavy consequence.
(Lafew)

The brains of my Cupid's knocked out, and I begin to love as an old man loves money, with no stomach.
(Clown)

The web of our life is a mingled yarn, good and ill together.
(First Lord)

...for I knew the young Count to be a dangerous and lascivious boy, who is a whale to virginity, and devours up all the fry it finds.
(Parolles)

There's place and means for every man alive.
(Parolles)

A scar nobly got, or a noble scar, is a good livery of honour.
(Lafew)

I am a man whom Fortune hath cruelly scratched.
(Parolles)

Though you are a fool and a knave you shall eat.
(Lafew)

Praising what is lost
Makes the remembrance dear.
(King)

For we are old, and on our quickest decrees
Th'inaudible and noiseless foot of time
Steals ere we can effect them.
(King)

I will buy me a son-in-law in a fair, and toll for this. I'll none of him.
(Lafew)

This woman's an easy glove, my lord: she goes off and on at pleasure.
(Lafew)

Mine eyes smell onions, I shall weep anon.
(Lafew)

TIMON OF ATHENS

In many ways *Timon of Athens* resembles *All's Well That Ends Well*: the date of composition and first performance are not definitively known; it is performed infrequently; Thomas Middleton is, by some, accredited with writing parts of it; and – even more so than *All's Well That Ends Well* – it is sometimes regarded as unfinished. Volumes have been written by academics exploring the uncertainties that surround the play, indecisively, but as far as we are concerned the important consensus is that it was written between 1606 and 1608, which places it immediately after *King Lear*, *Macbeth* and *Antony and Cleopatra* and just before *Coriolanus*. It makes sense to juxtapose it in time with *Coriolanus* as each play explores the response of their main protagonists to being rejected by the society – Roman and Athenian – in which, through Coriolanus' military prowess and Timon's financial generosity, each had played a leading role.

Coriolanus and Timon both abjure their native cities. What *Timon of Athens* especially brings to its readers and audience is a presentation – I use this word in preference to 'discussion' – of how wealth falsifies relationships, how greed corrupts and how Mammon rules. A play, it would seem, perfectly fitted for the ultra-capitalist times in which we live. And Nicholas Hytner's production at the National Theatre in 2012[60] underlined its contemporaneity by presenting Alcibiades and his army as a tented Occupy-style encampment, threateningly close to the opulence of a society in which Timon opens the Timon Room in an Art Gallery. Similarly in Trevor Nunn's production for the Young Vic in 1999 the cut throat, sycophantic world of the city was disturbingly well realized, and Nunn gave us Apemantus as a homeless victim of an inequitable society. The Young Vic production had Timon living in a battered car in a scrapyard, whereas in the

60   A production which featured a brilliant central performance by Simon Russell Beale.

169

Hytner production Timon is self-exiled to a cardboard city in a wasteland. Both directors have made it a relevant parable for our times.

It is, though, a play for all time, as a comment on the alienating effect of money, which is why Karl Marx wrote so much about *Timon of Athens*[61]. One of the points that Marx strenuously makes is that the power of money is disproportionate to the power of personal skills and abilities, and if someone gets drawn into worshipping money (s)he loses the capacity to be human – failing, for example, to be able to self-reflect and to love. Rapacity is all. Not only does (s)he lose touch with his/her common humanity but others too see him/her in a moneyed role only and not as an individual. The second main point that Marx makes is in calling gold "the universal agent of corruption and prostitution" and claiming that, "it gives [the individual] universal power as his private power". The word 'prostitution' incorporates women, but does not exclusively mean women: all people – indeed everything – can be procured by money. Timon addresses gold as "thou common whore of mankind". Marx agrees and, living today in times of bloated capitalism and increasing poverty, I see no fault in the Timon/Marx's belief.

The story in *Timon of Athens* is simple. Timon, when the play begins, is a wealthy and generous benefactor, sponsoring the arts, dispensing extravagant gifts to his friends and acquaintances and buying people out of their difficult situations. He had apparently not heard the warnings of his steward Flavius that he is running out of money, so is surprised when this eventuality comes to pass. However, he is confident that those to whom he has in the past been generous will help him out; he turns to them and one by one they refuse. Timon invites them to a banquet and, instead of the usual generous fare, he serves them warm water, throws it in their faces and throws his "mouth-friends... most smiling, smooth, detested parasites" out. We next meet Timon in self-imposed exile living in a cave in the woods outside Athens, nurtured by nature only. While digging, he finds a treasure trove and gives his new-found wealth away; not to the artists who had flattered him early in the play, but mainly to Alcibiades – who, like Timon, had previously done the

---

61   In *The German Ideology* (1846), *Outlines of the Critique of Political Economy* (1844) and *Economic and Philosophical Manuscripts* (1844).

state some service and then been rejected and exiled by the Athenian senators – in order to wage war against Athens. Most of the second part of the play is Timon's cynical rant about the perfidy of man and the corrupting power of money. The play ends abruptly with Timon writing his own epitaph expressing his hatred of mankind, his death being reported and Alcibiades invading Athens successfully but agreeing to a proportionate revenge on his enemies.

In so far as Timon is a once-great man who has fallen from a height of power and importance, he fulfils one of the Aristotelian criteria of being a tragic hero. But is there a learning process that produces wisdom involved in his descent, and is the audience emotionally wrung – the cathartic effect – by its identifying with the hero of the play and his suffering? This question behoves us to look at the character of Timon. It is remarkable that there is not an iota of personal backlog presented to us: we know of Macbeth's and Othello's and Antony's military achievements; we know of Hamlet's and Lear's family problems. Of Timon we know nothing, except that he is an over-generous benefactor to (almost) all and sundry. On that basis he is a confident extravert. Yet what motivates his generosity? Psychological theorists can – and do – have a field day exploring this. Maybe his munificence is all self-serving: he is desperate for recognition and acceptance. There is no indication of his sharing any intimacy in the play, so maybe there is an inherent fear of intimacy which fuels Timon and needs compensatory adulation. And so on. The real point, though, is that Timon is absolutely flat and one-dimensional. Shakespeare in the first part of *Timon of Athens* has given Timon one characteristic and has not otherwise bothered to individualise him. Arguably Timon has an even more simplistic persona in the second, dwelling-in-a-cave-outside-Athens, part of the play.

In this second part of the play he rails against everything and everybody: "I am Misanthropos and hate mankind." Eventually he acknowledges "one honest man", his faithful steward Flavius, but he pours scorn and contempt over everyone else. Greed and theft, for him, are inextricably bound into the human condition – but not just the human, for he sees the sun, the moon, the sea and the earth all as thieves; indeed "each thing's a thief". Such repetitive, single-track cynicism makes it difficult to feel empathy with Timon. There

171

is a lack of self-searching and consequent growth. He has gone from one extreme to another as a consequence of simply reacting to his loss of fortune and rejection. In both parts of the play one perceives little intelligence and understanding.

Timon has been likened, understandably, to both Coriolanus and Lear: all three are rejected by the society they serve and consequently wish to exact a certain revenge. But Coriolanus has a wife and, more especially, a mother to whom he can respond and with whom he can dialogue in human terms, and Lear is redeemed from his wrath and his madness by the love of Cordelia and the fidelity of Kent. This lack of any human relationship context is what makes Timon such an unsatisfactory character. Timon's thinking in both parts of the play is all too simple. The theme of the play – the corrupting power of money – is all too simple too and is presented, not explored, in an all-too-simple way. We are a long way from Shakespeare at his best.

And yet Herman Melville[62] saw *Timon of Athens* as one of Shakespeare's most profound plays, liking Timon to Hamlet, Lear and Iago as purveyors of truth and contrasting him with Richard III and Macbeth, whom he saw as one-dimensional, the one characterized only by a hump and the other by daggers. Even the most cursory look at the characterization and interactions of the other five characters within their plays – not to mention their self-searching soliloquys – will indicate what complete nonsense Melville is writing. I concur completely with Frank Kermode[63] when he calls *Timon of Athens* "a poor relation of the major tragedies".

If Timon is one-dimensional, what about the other characters? They are equally so. In fact most of them are not even given names – they are simply known as a poet, a painter, a jeweller, a merchant, lords and senators etc. We have a few names, Phyrnia and Timandra being Alcibiades' mistresses for example, but no real characterisation. A look at the three other main people in the play will demonstrate this.

---

62   In *Hawthorne and his Mosses* (1850), plus many references to Timon in his novel *The Confidence Man* (1857).
63   In *The Riverside Theatre* (1974).

I have mentioned Flavius, grudgingly acknowledged by Timon as a faithful steward, but there is no more to him than that. Apemantus is more interesting; not for any complex characterisation aspect – his being and philosophy do not change – but from the light he throws on Timon. In the list of characters he is labelled "a churlish philosopher", a stance he maintains throughout. In the first Act of the play Apemantus is, to Timon's face, powerfully critical of his 'friends' and their hypocrisies and in one of the more interesting scenes in the second part of the play, Apemantus points out to Timon: "the middle of humanity thou never knowest, but the extremity of both ends". There is a crude polarisation in Timon's behaviour. Apemantus' views are consistently cynical but, in practical terms, he has tempered his beliefs so that he is able to live within society. Timon has not been able to do that, mainly because his views have not been thought through. Apemantus tells him directly:

This is in thee a nature but infected,
A poor unmanly melancholy sprung
From change of future.

Timon only reacts: his cynicism is superficial, whereas that of Apemantus is a thought-through philosophical belief. Apemantus further underlines the shallowness of Timon.

The single other character of any note in *Timon of Athens* is Alcibiades, a military captain. Like Coriolanus and Othello he has done the state some service and, on the strength of this, appeals to the Senators on behalf of his friend who, in a moment of anger and hot blood and in defence of a besmirched reputation, has killed his decrier and thus been sentenced to death. Despite his service on behalf of Venice at Lacadaemon and Byzantium, and despite the wounds he has received and the pledges he gives for his friend's future conduct, Alcibiades' pleas are rejected; furthermore his insistence has angered the Senate and he is peremptorily banished. Such is his fury that Alcibiades turns his wrath against Athens and is given money by Timon in the second part of the play to wage war against the city. Apart from having two prostitutes in tow and being driven by rage, Alcibiades is not further individualised. What he does do, though, is to highlight the values of Athenian society and how it so easily rejects someone who has been its benefactor. To that extent it parallels and underlines the experience of Timon. There is no loyalty and human appreciation in the Athenian value-free world.

Athens is presented as a corrupted society: Alcibiades has been paid for his services and now nothing else matters; Timon had money, and now he has none no one will help him. Society has only financial obligations and values, and none other. The major question that arises from this is whether Timon truly is a victim of this rotten society or whether he colludes in its values, thereby making him an accomplice. I think this is the most controversial issue that the play throws up. And in so far as his one obsession throughout the play is money and there are no signs of any warmth in his relationships with his human contacts I think he has not only colluded in the values of Athens but has himself helped create them. Othello and Macbeth had wives; indeed Othello loved "not wisely but too well". Timon, by contrast, was unsuccessful in his buying of superficial friendship.

If Timon were simply a victim of fortune maybe some sympathy for him could be elicited. There is a discussion early in the play between the Painter and the Poet, the salient part of which is the first item on my Memorable Quotations appendix. This prepares us for the downfall of Timon and his subsequent treatment but I really don't think we can see Timon as an unfortunate victim of fate. If we believe that Timon played the role of generous benefactor as a way of buying affection – misguided as it was – and of increasing his own stature, boosting his ego, then manifestly a change of fortune is not a desperate calamity so much as a necessary hazard of a capitalist, money-centred way of life. If you accept the values of society, you rise and fall in keeping with those values.

All of which is an argument for the refusal to give Timon the accolade of 'tragic hero', although in the interests of fairness I should mention that there are other readings of *Timon of Athens*. Wilson Knight, for example, sees Timon as a Nietzschean superman, and others see him either as a mother figure distributing bounty or as a father figure using his wealth as a controlling mechanism. The truth is that, character-wise, Timon is such a flat, one-dimensional figure that you can read into him what you wish: there just is no psychological complexity and no self-awareness. Money and the

174

part it plays in his life is all we know about him.

This money factor justifies Marx using him as an example of the corrupting power of wealth and the rottenness of capitalism. It is as though *Timon of Athens* is less important as a play than as a symbol. As a play we can criticise it on many grounds: its lack of characterisation; the repetitive nature of both the theme and of Timon's ranting in the second part; the lack of vivid imagery or compassionate understanding and insight; and the apparently rushed ending. Can it as a symbol, though, compared with Eliot's *The Waste Land* or Beckett's *Waiting for Godot?*

No way! The titles of those two works represent a great poem and a great play, of which just about every word is telling. The title *Timon of Athens* may well serve as a symbol for extravagant expenditure and cynical misanthropy and thus be a comment on the corrupting power of money in society, but beyond the symbolic title there is little to commend the play, which is why directors like Nicholas Hytner have taken liberties with the play in an attempt to make it relevant: having Alcibiades as a leader of the Occupy movement rather than a military captain, for example, added a dimension of immediate relevance that justified its performance at the National in 2012. But the play *needs* to have value added. For me, because of how static and repetitive it is, I find it less satisfactory even than *All's Well That Ends Well*, but the part of Timon does attract great actors – Richard Pasco, David Suchet, Michael Pennington and, especially, Simon Russell Beale in recent years – and the play itself is a challenge for imaginative directors, so it is possible that production values might justify a visit to the theatre. Otherwise, for a serious discussion of the issues raised I would recommend reading Karl Marx.

Memorable Quotations From *Timon of Athens*

When Fortune in her shift and change of mood
Spurns down her late beloved, all his dependants
Which laboured after him to the mountain's top
Even on their knees and hands, let him slip down,
Not one accompanying his declining foot.
(Poet)

I am not of that feather to shake off
My friend when he must need me.
(Timon)

'Tis not enough to help the feeble up,
But to support him after.
(Timon)

He that loves to be flattered is worthy o'th'flatterer.
(Apemantus)

Great men should drink with harness on their throats.
(Apemantus)

Why, I have often wished myself poorer, that I might come nearer to you.
(Timon)

Men shut their doors against a setting sun.
(Apemantus)

What needs these feasts, pomps and vainglories?
(Apemantus)

Ah, when the means are gone that buy this praise,
The breath is gone whereof this praise is made.
(Flavius)

Who can call him his friend
That dips in the same dish?
(First Stranger)

Who bates mine honour shall not know my coin.
(Sempronius)

Nothing emboldens sin so much as mercy.
(First Senator)

He's truly valiant that can wisely suffer
The worst that man can breathe.
(First Senator)

But who is man that is not angry?
(Alcibiades)

The swallow follows not summer more willingly than we your lordship.
(Second Lord)

You knot of mouth-friends!...
You fools of fortune, trencher-friends, time's flies.
(Timon)

We have seen better days.
(Flavius)

This yellow slave
Will knit and break religions...
(Timon)

I am Misanthropos, and hate mankind.
(Timon)

Pity not honoured age for his white beard;
He is an usurer.
(Timon)

Thou art a slave, whom Fortune's tender arm
With favour never clasped, but bred a dog.
(Timon)

(Looks at the gold)
O thou sweet king-killer, and dear divorce
'Twixt natural son and sire.
(Timon)

Trust not the physican,
His antidotes are poison, and he slays
Moe than you rob…
The sun's a thief… the moon's an arrant thief…
The sea's a thief… the earth's a thief
…each thing's a thief…
(Timon)

Life's uncertain voyage.
(Timon)

Crimes, like lands,
Are not inherited.
(First Senator)

And I will use the olive with my sword.
(Alcibiades)

TWELFTH NIGHT

It is a real joy to turn to *Twelfth Night* after the considerably less accomplished plays *All's Well That Ends Well* and *Timon of Athens*. Here is a play that sings with poetry and has each character, including the minor ones, clearly delineated. I cannot claim to be a linguistics expert, but the quality of the writing in *Twelfth Night* is palpably so vastly superior to much of that of *All's Well That Ends Well* and almost all of the ranting of *Timon of Athens*: Middleton indisputably had a large hand in both of them.

Twelfth Night is truly a delightful play. It is certainly a serious contender – along with *A Midsummer Night's Dream* and *Romeo and Juliet* – to be the first Shakespeare play for your seven-year-old child to see. The confusion, fun and romance all speak in its favour, as does the fact that there is no need to bowdlerise[64] it – the only sexual reference, when Malvolio persuades himself by reference to the way Olivia shapes her letters that she really is the author of the letter he has received, would be lost on children. The play would in fact have initially been seen on Twelfth Night[65] as a family post-Christmas entertainment. It is true that the play was initially called *What You Will*, but the title had been stolen by fellow dramatist John Marston before Shakespeare had completed his play, which meant that the occasion determined the title.

A shipwreck is the significant background to the play, a shipwreck in which identical twins Viola and Sebastian are both rescued, though

64   To bowdlerise is to censor work to make it appropriate for the whole family; a term named after Thomas Bowdler who published *The Family Shakespeare* on July 11th 1754.
65   It is possible that *Twelfth Night* was played before the court at Whitehall Palace on Twelfth Night 1601, but the first recorded performance was at Candlemas, February 2nd 1602.

each believes the other has drowned. Viola finds herself in Illyria where the Duke is hopelessly in love with Olivia, who rejects all his advances as she is in mourning for her father and brother who both died a year or so previously. In order to get by as a woman in a strange land Viola disguises herself as a eunuch (Cesario) and finds employment in the Duke's service. Viola's main function is to deliver messages to Olivia from the Duke, but Olivia falls in love with the go-between, believing Viola to be the young man Cesario. The Duke too has conceived a great affection for 'Cesario' and wishes he were a girl, while at the same time Viola has fallen in love with the Duke! This identity (and love) confusion comes to a head when Sebastian eventually arrives on the island. It is all eventually happily resolved with the Duke and Olivia each ending up with a partner of the appropriate sex!

There is a more than interesting subplot too, centred around Olivia's household. Her kinsman Sir Toby Belch is a member thereof, and he likes his drink and general roistering. In this he is accompanied by his friend Sir Andrew Aguecheek, who has been deluded by Sir Toby (shades of Iago and Roderigo) into thinking that he is in with a chance of successfully wooing Olivia. The behaviour of these two runs counter to the puritan instincts of Olivia's officious steward, Malvolio, so a trick, instituted by Olivia's serving woman Maria, is played on Malvolio. A letter purporting to be from Olivia, expressing her love for Malvolio, is dropped in front of him, exhorting him to dress and behave strangely: this he does and is consequently deemed mad and placed in solitary confinement. Feste, the Clown or the Fool, is also a significant part of Olivia's household, but more of his significance (mainly in the tone rather than the plot of the play) later.

Gender and identity cause the confusion in *Twelfth Night*. It is a ploy used by Shakespeare in so many of his plays as female characters, usually for reasons of security and safe passage (see Portia, Nerissa and Jessica in *The Merchant of Venice*, Rosalind in *As You Like It* and Imogen in *Cymbeline*) disguise themselves as males. Of course it is especially dramatically effective as – because until December 1661 it was thought morally unacceptable for women to act in the theatre – Shakespeare's females were all played by boys. Inevitably questions of sexual identity arise and, as I shall discuss later, in *Twelfth Night* at least this raises interesting issues.

Not only is cross-dressing a feature of this and other plays, but so too are many other aspects of *Twelfth Night*. Shipwrecks, for example, are key devices in *Pericles* and *The Tempest*. Mostly, though, the references in *Twelfth Night* look back to Shakespeare's earlier plays: the confusion brought about by identical twins was first used in *The Comedy of Errors*, Sir Toby Belch has similarities with Sir John Falstaff and Sir Andrew Aguecheek has a deal in common with Slender in *The Merry Wives of Windsor*.

So Shakespeare is actually working with many familiar ideas and concepts, which might well account for the apparent confidence in the writing of *Twelfth Night*, in which he scarcely puts a foot wrong. Some of Shakespeare's comedy and puns have dated, but not in this play. Starting with the names, we immediately have an insight into the characters of Toby Belch and Andrew Aguecheek, the one a *bon viveur* and the other a sickly weed. Aguecheek is particularly pathetic, not only in his totally misplaced belief that Olivia might see him as a suitable suitor but in his duel with whom he saw as an unwilling Cesario/Viola, but who turned out to be a more than willing and competent Sebastian. So name, character and action all provide humour, but it is especially his badinage with Sir Toby that makes Aguecheek – though plot-wise scarcely significant – a memorable part of *Twelfth Night*.

But in no sense is *Twelfth Night* character-driven. Such is the tone of the play from the beginning that we know there are going to be complications of plot, but that, despite these, we are moving inevitably towards a happy ending. Both Duke Orsino and Olivia seem to be playing a role: the one of the unrequited lover, the other of someone deep in mourning. The play opens with the "if music be the food of love" speech and Orlando requesting "excess of it": he is clearly indulging himself in his feelings of love and eloquently rhapsodising thereon. Similarly Olivia, and again we are told in the very first scene of *Twelfth Night*, has vowed to wear a mourning veil for another seven years in response to her brother's death which happened a year ago. Eight years of mourning for a brother! There is either the whiff of incest here or Olivia, like Duke Orsino, is enjoying dramatising her feelings. Clearly it is the latter.

181

Whereas in tragedy we expect the protagonists to learn through suffering, in comedy no such insights are gained. What happens, though, in *Twelfth Night* is that Olivia and the Duke stop play-acting when genuine feelings of affection are aroused as a result of personal meetings and interactions. Olivia especially is quick to drop her pose: one meeting with Viola, acting as the go-between Cesario, is enough for her to forget – and never again mention – her dead brother: she unveils herself to the youth who is supposed to "unfold the passion" of Orsino's love, chats merrily with him and, very forwardly, sends Malvolio after Cesario to give him a ring, thus indicating her attraction to him. I don't think either the Duke or Olivia has come to any profound understanding about the nature of love and relationships, but they do cast off their indulgent adolescent affectations and respond honestly and hormonally to real contact.

I nearly concluded that last paragraph by writing "real contact with real people", but of course, the person (and it is only one!) the Duke and Olivia fall for is not a real person, in the sense of the dressed-up Viola not being what (s)he seems to be. So the question then becomes: "Does *Twelfth Night* have anything to contribute on the subject of gender identity and sexuality?" The Duke's relationship with Viola is fairly straightforward: he recognizes that Viola/Cesario possesses "all [that] is semblative a woman's part", but is obsessed with his love for Olivia: "Make no compare," he boasts, "Between that love a woman can bear me / And that I owe Olivia." Yet, at the end of the play, having realised that he really does stand nowhere with regard to wooing and marrying Olivia, he quite happily takes Viola's hand, knowing full well that she has fallen for him. Granted that there has been a good deal of emotional posing taking place, it seems nonetheless that this relationship can safely be described as orthodox heterosexual.

When it comes to the relationship between Olivia and Viola/Cesario, though, it is not at all so straightforward. Olivia falls immediately for Cesario who, though dressed as a boy, resembles a girl. All clearly indicative of (on Olivia's part) a possible female/female relationship. Of course she marries the male twin and an orthodox respectability is maintained, but there has been an undoubted frisson between the two women. Now it is true that having boys play the female parts in his plays gives Shakespeare the possibility of having fun with gender disguises and identity, but he makes the most of this necessity and teases us all with the inherent confusion thereof. And it is this teasing that demonstrates Shakespeare's playfulness and also his open-mindedness. All of us are somewhere along a spectrum which has exclusive heterosexuality at one end and exclusive homosexuality at the other end, and there are probably only a handful of people in the whole world who occupy the extreme positions. I think Shakespeare in *Twelfth Night* in particular is opening minds to possibilities. Of course he is not a gay rights campaigner, but I reckon that if he were alive today he would be in favour of gay marriage.

Fundamentally, though, this gender confusion is simply an aspect of the plot, a plot much of whose fun revolves around Viola's cross-dressing and the confusion caused by it. *Twelfth Night* is, however, mainly a play to delight and enjoy. I will finish this essay by looking at the contributions Feste and music make to further create the delight of the play, but before I do that I want to examine the one aspect of the play which strikes a dissonant note – the treatment of Malvolio.

For Maria, Sir Toby, Sir Andrew and Fabian the gulling of Malvolio provides immense fun, and we the audience share in the fun as a pompous bubble is pricked. But there is a question as to whether Malvolio deserves the treatment he receives. In *Twelfth Night* Malvolio is given two tasks by Olivia: one is to run after Viola/Cesario with a ring and the second is to tell Sir Toby and his carousing friends that if he cannot "separate yourself and your misdemeanours" he must leave her house. It is this second task which arouses Sir Toby's wrath and causes Maria to write the letter, purporting to be from Olivia and to express her love for him, that makes a fool of Malvolio, causing him to be locked up, treated as a madman and, in the only dissonant note in the play, leads to his final angry threat: "I'll be revenged on the whole pack of you."

Now, if it were only carrying out his duty that occasioned the cruel trick played on Malvolio, a good deal of unease about the justness of his punishment would be acceptable. Indeed Kenneth Muir[66] quotes Charles Lamb's description of Malvolio as played by Bentley: "...

---

66   In *Shakespeare's Comic Sequence*, 1979.

his pride, or his gravity (call it which you will), is inherent and native to the man, not mock or affected, which latter only are the fit objects to excite laughter… His bearing is lofty, a little above his station, but probably not much above his deserts. We see no reason why he should not have been brave, honourable, accomplished." There is more too, all basically questioning what is seen as the disproportionate humiliation of Malvolio, and along those lines lies the "poor, unjustly fooled, Malvolio" school of thought.

But those comments were based on a single interpretation of Malvolio's character. What we need to do is look at the text, and there we find the material for an entirely different argument, one which indicates how suitable *is* the treatment meted out to Malvolio. Right from the first moment we meet Malvolio Olivia gives us her perspective on him, a perspective which is supported by everything that follows: Olivia has asked Malvolio to comment on the wit of the Clown and from a disdainful position of assumed superiority he is scornful of the "barren rascal", and Olivia reprehends Malvolio for his lack of generosity of spirit and pins his character down with "O, you are sick of self-love, Malvolio." And this being "sick with self-love" manifests itself throughout *Twelfth Night*. After Malvolio has reprimanded Sir Toby, Sir Andrew and Maria for their excessive carousing (though, admittedly, he had been asked by Olivia to rebuke Sir Toby), Maria follows the same train of response to Malvolio as had Olivia: she calls him "a time-pleaser, an affectioned ass" and describes him as being "so crammed, as he thinks, with excellencies, that it is his ground of faith that all that look on him love him". So self-regarding, so full of himself, so pompously self-inflated! Such a man is riding for a fall. His self-important bubble needs to be pricked, and that deflation is well warranted.

Which is why most of the audience will accept, I believe, the trick Maria plays on Malvolio. The trick is not played on the undeserving. And notice how Malvolio responds to the (apparent) love-letter from Olivia that he finds – indeed even before he finds the letter he is musing on being "Count Malvolio". Nowhere is there any mention of any reciprocal love or indeed affection he might have for Olivia. He sees greatness as having been thrust upon him and just imagines the power and status he will have as "Count Malvolio", and the superiority he will then have to Sir Toby. He boasts: "I am not of your element." It is self-preening to the nth degree, meriting Sir Toby's description of him as "an overweening rogue". Yes indeed, he is made a fool of: "there was never man so notoriously abused," he claims. It could be argued that imprisoning him as a madman takes the joke too far, and as one of the main planks for my argument as to the relevance of Shakespeare for today is his all-encompassing generosity of spirit, there is something in that argument. But I fail to see anything redeeming in the character of Malvolio. Just as Iago deserves to die, so Malvolio deserves to be ridiculed mercilessly.

I have come almost to the end of my musings on *Twelfth Night* so it really is time to write about the most important personage in the play – most important as he sets the overall mood of the play. I refer to the Clown, also known as Feste the Jester. His individualised character is not significant but he is one of Shakespeare's great creations; one of Shakespeare's two great fools, the other being King Lear's companion. Each of these fools has the art and wit to gain the respect and affection of their employers[67]. We are indebted to Feste for the expression "the whirligig of time" and the wry, perceptive precision of comments such as "Many a good hanging prevents a bad marriage." Olivia approves of his wit and insights – "thou speakest well of fools" – and contrasts Feste's words with the sour, uncharitable put-downs of Malvolio.

Where Feste assumes his greatest significance, though, is through his songs. There are great songs in many Shakespeare plays – Ariel's song in *The Tempest* and *Fear no more the heat of the Sun* in *Cymbeline* for example – but there are three exquisite songs in *Twelfth Night*, full of wit and a wry melancholy; memorable songs all. The play begins with Orsino calling for music and it ends with a song – the "hey ho, the wind and the rain" song. *Twelfth Night* is the most lyrical and musical of Shakespeare's plays. The words and the rhythm of the songs almost demand no music. There is no need for a clever musician to show off his/her talents and drown the words with grandiose tunes or orchestration: the simpler the accompanying music the better, for the words and their sentiments are the essence of *Twelfth Night*. The songs are delightful. *Twelfth Night* is truly a delightful play.

---

67   Feste is employed by Olivia, but he moves between her household and that of Orsino.

Memorable Quotations From *Twelfth Night*

If music be the food of love, play on;
Give me excess of it, that, surfeiting,
The appetite may sicken, and so to die.
That strain again! it had a dying fall.
(Duke)

Methinks sometimes I have no more wit than a Christian or an ordinary
man has; but I am a great eater of beef, and I believe that does harm to my
wit.
(Sir Andrew Aguecheek)

I would I had bestowed that time in the tongues that I have in fencing,
dancing and bear-bating. O! had I but followed the arts.
(Sir Andrew Aguecheek)

Many a good hanging prevents a bad marriage.
(Clown)

Lady, you are the cruell'st she alive
If you will lead these graces to the grave
And leave the world no copy.
(Viola)

Make me a willow cabin at your gate.
(Viola)

For she did speak in starts distractedly…
(Viola)

O mistress mine! where are you roaming?
O! stay and hear; your true love's coming...
Trip no further, pretty sweeting;
Journeys end in lovers meeting,
Every wise man's son doth know.
What is love? 'tis not hereafter;
Present mirth hath present laughter...
Then come kiss me, sweet and twenty,
Youth's a stuff will not endure.
(Clown)

Have you no wit, manners, nor honesty, but to gabble like tinkers at this time of night? Do ye make an ale-house of my lady's house...?
(Malvolio)

Dost thou think, because thou art virtuous, there shall be no more cakes and ale?
(Sir Toby Belch)

Marry, sir, sometimes he is a kind of puritan.
(Maria)
O, if I thought that, I'd beat him like a dog!
(Sir Andrew Aguecheek)

For such as I am all true lovers are;
Unstaid and skittish in all motions else,
Save in the constant image of the creature
That is belov'd.
(Duke)

Our fancies are more giddy and unfirm,
More longing, wavering, sooner lost and won
Than woman's are.
(Duke)

Come away, come away, death,
And in sad cypress let me be laid;
Fly away, fly away, breath:
I am slain by a fair cruel maid.
(Clown)

This fellow is wise enough to play the fool,
And to do that well craves a kind of wit.
(Viola)

She sat like patience on a monument,
Smiling at grief.
(Viola)

But be not afraid of greatness: some men are born great, some achieve
greatness, and some have greatness thrust upon them.
(Malvolio)

Love sought is good, but giv'n unsought better.
(Olivia)

Why, this is very midsummer madness.
(Olivia)

In nature there's no blemish but the mind;
None else can be call'd deform'd but the unkind.
(Antonio)

O he's drunk, Sir Toby, an hour agone; his eyes were set at eight
i'th'morning.
(Clown)

And thus the whirligig of time brings in his revenges.
(Clown)

I'll be revenged on the whole pack of you.
(Malvolio)

When that I was and a little tiny boy,
With hey, ho, the wind and the rain;
A foolish thing was but a toy,
For the rain it raineth every day…
A great while ago the world begun,
With hey, ho, the wind and the rain;
But that's all one, our play is done,
And we'll strive to please you every day.
(Clown)

JULIUS CAESAR

From the internal evidence of the verse and from contemporary comments it would appear that *Julius Caesar* was written in 1599. Eighteen plays were written before it and eighteen plays after, so numerically it very much marks the midpoint of Shakespeare's career, but, more than this, it ushers in the great series of plays that have put Shakespeare firmly in position as the world's number one dramatist. It is probably, after *Hamlet*, the play most quoted from and it deals with the universal themes of political power and tyranny, personal loyalty and patriotism, and love. It comments on the fickleness and persuadeability of crowds and on the ultimate need for order.

Julius Caesar was written at a time when the queen had only four years to live and, with no heir to succeed her, civil strife and disorder were more than merely a possibility. Thus the play was relevant to its times, but it is a play for all time. Recently – in 2012 – there have been both all-black and all-female productions of the play. I could not get tickets for the all-female production, but saw the all-black production at Stratford: set in Africa, it had a good deal to say of relevance to contemporary African politics. I find it interesting too that John Wilkes Booth, the man who assassinated President Lincoln at Ford's Theatre, Washington on April 14th 1865, had played Mark Antony in a production of *Julius Caesar* at the New York Winter Gardens the previous year – a production which raised funds for the statue of Shakespeare which is still to be seen in Central Park.

Be that as it may, *Julius Caesar* begins the sequence of wonderful plays written in the second part of Shakespeare's creative life. The story was taken from Thomas North's translation of Plutarch's *Lives*. Whereas Enobarbus' great description of Cleopatra arriving on her barge to meet Mark Antony is taken pretty accurately from North, the two great (funeral) orations here are very much Shakespeare's. His stagecraft is very much in evidence too as he compresses events to make it appear that they all took place on the same day: whereas the feast of Lupercal, when the play begins, was 15th February, the assassination took place a month later on the Ides of March, Caesar's will was read three days after the assassination and the burial then took place on 20th March. And Octavius Caesar did not arrive in Rome until May. So liberties were taken with time[68] – to superb dramatic effect. Shakespeare too makes Caesar deaf in the left ear, but for the most part, the story is Plutarch's/North's. It is, of course, what Shakespeare does with the story and the words he uses to tell it that matters.

So what is the story? At the beginning we learn that the all-powerful, all-conquering Caesar is being feted by the people in the marketplace, but that not everyone is happy about this, and people's representatives, the tribunes, are pulling down portraits of Caesar. We later learn that Caesar was offered, by Mark Antony on behalf of the people, a crown of kingship three times, which he – apparently reluctantly and feigning modesty – refused. He also fainted. Cassius is concerned that Caesar has too much power and will the next day, when it is offered to him by the Senate, take the crown. Hence his organisation of the conspiracy to assassinate Caesar, and his keenness to have the honourable Brutus join the murdering faction. Brutus is persuaded to do so, although Caesar is his friend, for the good of Rome. Caesar has been warned by a Soothsayer to beware the Ides of March and his wife Calphurnia has had disturbing dreams which could foretell her husband's assassination. Caesar's pride, though, eventually overrules all other considerations and he goes to the Capitol and is duly assassinated, with all the conspirators, including Brutus, putting the knife in. The conspirators then have to deal with an enraged Mark Antony, and it is Brutus who persuades his fellow murderers to save Antony's life and indeed to permit Antony to speak after him at Caesar's funeral. Mark Antony's speech arouses riots and chaos in Rome, and Brutus and Cassius have to flee for their safety. Caesar's great-nephew Octavius (proclaimed by Caesar as his heir) unites with Antony and their forces meet with those of Brutus and Cassius at Philippi. Before the battle Brutus and Cassius

---

68   As Shakespeare did similarly in *Othello* with its double-time sequence.

have quarrelled, though this has been resolved, and also Caesar's ghost has appeared to Brutus. Cassius and Brutus are both defeated and commit suicide, Mark Antony eulogises Brutus as "the noblest Roman of them all" and he and Octavius (and Lepidus) are left to rule Rome and restore order.

Julius Caesar is the most character-centred of all Shakespeare's plays. There is very clear delineation of the minor characters, but it is the four major characters – Caesar, Mark Antony, Cassius and Brutus – that I wish initially to focus on. (The character of Octavius is far more developed in *Antony and Cleopatra*, where we also hear much more about Lepidus, memorably described in this play by Mark Antony as "a slight, unmeritable man, meet to be sent on errands".) The first thing to note is that there are no villains in *Julius Caesar*: rather alarmingly, Dante in his *Divine Comedy* places Cassius and Brutus, along with Judas Iscariot, in his lowest circle of Hell[69], but I am completely in agreement with A. C. Bradley and his assertion that in *Julius Caesar* "everybody means well".

Writing in *The Political Characters in Shakespeare* (1945), John Palmer gives what is for me a very helpful insight into the way Shakespeare presents characters in *Julius Caesar*: "He has his characters alive and fully-formed in his mind. He takes for granted their primary qualities... They do not come alive, feature by feature. They spring upon the stage in full career." Of course when the playwright's characters are known to most of the audience, although as a writer you may hope to modify any preconceived ideas held about them, you are not going to turn these ideas completely on their heads, so such an approach is the most obvious one. And it certainly works in *Julius Caesar*, especially with Caesar himself, for as Palmer points out: "Caesar's greatness is assumed throughout the play."[70] From the

69   Dante gives no reason, but presumably this is for betrayal and treason, as with Judas.
70   Not everyone agrees with my comments about Caesar and the conspirators. George Bernard Shaw, in the *Saturday Review* in 1898, reviewing Beerbohm Tree's production of *Julius Caesar* and – as ever – anxious to discredit Shakespeare, writes: "It is impossible for even the most judicially minded critic to look without revulsion of indignant contempt at this travestying of a great man as a silly braggart, whilst the pitiful gang of mischief-makers who destroyed

first scene when the tribunes, Flavius and Marullus, disillusioned supporters of the defeated Pompey, encourage the crowd to tear down the pictures celebrating Caesar's triumphs, to Antony's last one-word description of Caesar in his final speech – that word is "great" – there is no denying the esteem in which Caesar is held by most of Rome. He had defeated both Pompey and his sons so there was likely to be a period of peace; he had "brought many captives home to Rome" which had added to the general coffers; a statue had been erected to him in the Capitol inscribed "to the demi-god"; and his will was generous to the people of Rome.

That is one – vastly important – aspect of Caesar. Shakespeare also emphasizes the human, and weaker, aspect of Caesar. (And I think it interesting that of the four features of Caesar's I listed in the last sentence of the last paragraph, Shakespeare mentions the first only through the negative comments of the tribunes and the third not at all.) We hear of Caesar's fainting in public; from Cassius we learn of the challenge Caesar gave about swimming in the Tiber to a particular point and how Cassius, having taken up the challenge, had to rescue him from the waves; how Caesar cried out "as a sick girl"; and we learn that he is deaf in one ear. Human frailties all, and yet "this man hath become a god". He has not succeeded in fathering a son to continue his rule, putting the blame for this on his wife Calphurnia's barrenness, but he does listen to her dream and its interpretation and, on a human level, initially responds by withdrawing from his meeting with the Senate[71], only to be persuaded by Decius, invoking the Senate being likely to interpret Caesar's non-attendance as being a result of his fear, to change his mind. Pride leads him to his assassination, a pride that we have previously witnessed when he boasts of being "as constant as the northern star" and when he asserts that "What touches us ourself shall be last served." There is too a distinction, not quite fully maintained, between Caesar as ruler and Caesar as an individual, by the former speaking in the third person and the latter in the first. What we have, though, is a wonderfully complex figure, full of private doubt and public certainty.

---

him are lauded as statesmen and patriots." Not everything Shaw wrote is contestable, however. In another context he disparagingly wrote: "All men mean well." That is in tune with my feelings about Brutus.

71   Notice "for he is superstitious grown of late " (Cassius).

Yet Caesar is not the only character in this play to be so fully imagined. There is also Mark Antony. We learn that he loves plays and music; that he "revels long o' nights" – a playboy, it would seem, and yet these characteristics are not in evidence in *Julius Caesar*, though they do come to the fore in *Antony and Cleopatra*. His oratory is unsurpassed as, movingly responding and speaking from the heart, he incites the mob to revenge the death of Caesar, though he claims to be "no orator, as Brutus is, / But, as you know me all, a plain blunt man". Love and loyalty, both to Caesar and Rome, are the keynotes in Antony's character. Plus generalship: there is no doubt as to who is the leader of the Antony/Octavius/Lepidus triumvirate. He leads his army into battle and he eulogises Brutus – if we were seeking a hero in *Julius Caesar* then Mark Antony might well fill the bill, but the play cannot be seen in black-and-white terms. There are serious political issues being examined and Mark Antony and his character contribute to that examination – and he did betray the trust Brutus placed in him.

Had Cassius had his way, Antony would have died along with Caesar. Cassius is the main instigator of the plot to kill Caesar, but he needs Brutus on board, and in order to achieve this he, sometimes protestingly, always defers to Brutus. The question that will always hang over Cassius is whether he led the conspiracy against Caesar out of envy or out of a genuine belief that such a conspiracy was necessary for the good of Rome. Plutarch describes Cassius as "hot, choleric and cruel", and Shakespeare gives evidence of these character traits, most especially in the quarrel scene between Cassius and Brutus before the battle of Philippi, when his first words to Brutus are "most noble brother, you have done me wrong". Shakespeare adds many more characteristics, though. Undoubtedly Cassius is envious of the power of Caesar and sees himself as at least an equal – witness the swimming-in-the-Tiber episode, and his calling Caesar "a man of such a feeble temper" who is now bestriding the world like a Colossus. There is something not quite honest about him: Caesar (who had historically forgiven both Cassius and Brutus for their earlier fighting on the side of Pompey) now distrusts him: he is the man "with a lean and hungry look", a dangerous reader and thinker who scornfully "looks quite through the deeds of men". An envious, unsmiling man. He piles pressure on Brutus to join the conspiracy by having supportive letters thrown through his window, purporting to have come from a wide range of Roman citizens but in reality having emanated from Cassius and his fellow conspirators.

And yet he has to stand by while Brutus wrecks all his plans vis-à-vis Mark Antony and at Philippi. Also in the latter stages of *Julius Caesar* Shakespeare gives him other human qualities: his anger with Brutus is soon over and he talks of having inherited his "rash humour" from his mother. We also learn that it is his birthday, and the man who fervently claimed, "the fault, dear Brutus, is not in our stars, but in ourselves" sees omens in departing eagles and the neatness of dying on his birthday. In death, too, he frees his slave Pindarus. Another complex and fascinating character, who is also given some wonderful verse to speak. The audience is always left with Antony's verdict that except for Brutus, all the other conspirators (obviously including Cassius) acted out of envy. Of course there is truth in that, but Cassius is so much more than any such simplification.

We now come to the fourth and arguably the most interesting of *Julius Caesar*'s protagonists: Brutus, who has four times more lines to speak than does Caesar, which has led some critics to suggest that the play can be split into two parts, the first three Acts being the tragedy of Caesar and the last two Acts the tragedy of Brutus. Well, maybe... Always remembered as "the noblest Roman of them all", I want to challenge that soubriquet. Granted that Brutus does agonise about the killing of Caesar. Granted that, eventually, he shares his concerns with his wife Portia, and she at the end of the play commits suicide by swallowing fire, apparently unable to endure her husband's absence: a good marriage, then. It is true also that he is gentle and caring towards his boy servant Lucius. All these betoken a good man. Perhaps too his saving of Mark Antony's life – "Let us be sacrificers, but not butchers" – indicates a sound, moral man; the kind of man who receives unbidden loyalty: "My heart doth joy that yet in all my life / I found no man but he was true to me."

And yet, and yet, and yet... Every political decision Brutus makes, he gets wrong. Allowing Antony to live; allowing Antony to follow him in speaking at Caesar's funeral; the decision to march towards

Philippi and meet the enemy there. All these decisions were against the wishes of Cassius, and all were wrong. Yet his one reason for agreeing to the assassination of Caesar was that it was for the good of Rome. How can such an apparently politically naive and incompetent in political thinking know what is for the good of Rome? In fact the consequences are civil strife and the eventual breakup of the Roman Empire. Brutus is no Harold Wilson, no shrewd political thinker.

And his human values are most questionable. He loved Caesar – a mutual feeling as shown by Caesar's horror-stricken and amazed "Et tu, Brute" as he falls – and yet his justification for killing Caesar was that he loved Rome more than he loved Caesar. One is inexorably reminded of E. M. Forster's dictum that "if I had to choose between betraying my country and my friend, I hope I should have the guts to betray my country". Yes! Friendship and love are the cast-iron hallmarks of all that is best is human society, and Brutus rejects them for the sake of a political cause he never fully understands and whose consequences he certainly does not foresee. As a man he hides behind morality and rationality, foolishly believing that the Roman crowd will take on board his sensible argument as to why Caesar had to die. In his argument with Cassius in Act 4 Scene 3 he tenaciously tries to inhabit the moral high ground. Finally, though, notice how he responds to the death of his wife Portia – with a trained stoicism!

Why, farewell Portia. We must die, Messala.
With meditating that she must die once,
I have the patience to endure it now.

I regard that as sanctimonious bullshit. This man has betrayed his friend Caesar and now he is suppressing his grief for his wife. As a friend and lover, as an orator, as a practical politician – indeed as an overall human being who both knows the time of day and what matters in life – Mark Antony surpasses Brutus in every way.

It is, though, through the character of Brutus that Shakespeare enables us to engage with the complexity of political issues. Before we go there, however, I want to comment briefly on the characterisations of the more minor figures in *Julius Caesar*. The women play no part at all in the political events, but each is clearly individualised and has a distinctive relationship with her husband. Portia knows that as Cato's daughter she is a woman "well-reputed", and she has demonstrated her strength by wounding herself voluntarily in the thigh. She knows that Brutus has "some sick offence within [his] mind" and she implores him on her knees as an equal in their marriage to tell her what is going on. Brutus knows what a "worthy wife" she is and, though interrupted at this moment of pleading, he does inform her later of the conspiracy. Finally, of course, she commits suicide by swallowing fire, grieved by her lengthy absence from her husband and not sharing his life. A strong, bold woman, and respected by Cassius too. Yet she is irrelevant to the basic political plot. Shakespeare need not have included her, or he could have made her a mere cypher, but he chooses to make her live.

Calphurnia, Caesar's wife, is similarly presented. We know that she is barren and that the personal/superstitious part of Caesar instructs her to stand where she may be touched by Antony as he speeds past in the chase, as that may shake off her "sterile curse" [72]. We are also told of her bloody dreams the night before the assassination. The first of these is irrelevant to the plotting, as is the second – indeed with regard to the dream it could have easily been simply reported. Caesar's engagement in dialogue with Calphurnia adds nothing to the political plotting. But it all throws more light on the superstitious nature of Caesar the man, and adds to the complete authenticity of the story. Character individuation is found throughout *Julius Caesar*. Perhaps Shakespeare was given the material for this by Plutarch and North, but he chooses to use it fully. Other minor characters like Casca and the boy Lucius also come individually to life – even Cinna the poet, mistaken initially for Cinna the conspirator, comes to life as he is ultimately killed "for his bad verses".

This killing of Cinna the poet is an example of the fickle nature of the mob and what can happen when it gets out of control. Flavius and Marullus have tried unsuccessfully to move them to revolt at the outset of *Julius Caesar*, but soon "this common body" is manipulated like the "vagabond flag upon the stream"[73], both by Brutus and Mark Antony as they speak at Caesar's funeral. Caesar himself

---

72   Maybe mentioned (but not emphasised) because of there being no natural successor to Caesar – and therefore relevant to the plot.
73   The words of Octavius Caesar in *Antony and Cleopatra*.

had previously had the crowd eating out of his hand when Antony offered him the crown in the marketplace. We saw people-power in *Coriolanus*, and it verged on anarchy there, but here is real anarchy as Cinna the poet is murdered and Brutus and Cassius and the whole shebang of the conspirators are driven out of Rome, fleeing for their lives. Civil war ensues and Rome and the Roman Empire will never be the same again.

This issue of how to incorporate dissent within a civilised democracy is the central issue of the play. On one hand you have Caesar acting as an autocrat, condemning Flavius and Marullus to death without trial and also refusing to be swayed by the appeals of Cassius, Brutus and his brother Metellus Cimber for the repeal of Publius Cimber's banishment. On the other hand you have a wild mob. Striving for a balance between control and freedom, between order and anarchy, between power and justice still dogs all political landscapes and even a partially satisfactory solution has yet to be found. Order is always important for Shakespeare, and at no time more so than in 1599 when there was no clear successor to Elizabeth I.

As ever Shakespeare gives us no answers, though he does give a clear indication as to where his thinking is leaning, which is on the side of order. But *Julius Caesar* is fundamentally about characters and human values. The four main protagonists are so fully drawn that it would be wrong to characterise them as representing power, loyalty, envy and rationality respectively – there is so much more to each of them than one glib epithet. It is fair, though, I contend, to suggest that when it comes to a comparison between Brutus and Antony, both close friends of Caesar, Shakespeare comes down unerringly on the side of Antony; personal loyalty being a stronger human value than rational thought. Can we blame Brutus for having no imagination, no political foresight as to the consequences of his actions? Probably, but even those who might put up a strong defence of Brutus' behaviour will, I think, have to concede that he was in fact not "the noblest Roman of them all", and that the humanity of Mark Antony is the abiding memory we have of this wonderful, human-centred play.

Memorable Quotations From *Julius Caesar*

When Caesar says, "Do this," it is performed.
(Antony)

Beware the Ides of March.
(Soothsayer)

For let the gods so speed me as I love
The name of honour more than I fear death.
(Brutus)

Why man, he doth bestride the narrow world
Like a Colossus, and we petty men
Walk under his huge legs, and peep about
To find ourselves dishonourable graves.
The fault, dear Brutus, is not in our stars,
But in ourselves, that we are underlings.
(Cassius)

Let me have men about me that are fat,
Sleek-headed men, and such as sleep a-nights.
Yond Cassius has a lean and hungry look;
He thinks too much. Such men are dangerous.
(Caesar)

...for mine own part, it was Greek to me.
(Casca)

It is the bright day that brings forth the adder.
(Brutus)

Between the acting of a dreadful thing
And the first motion, all the interim is
Like a phantasma, or a hideous dream.
(Brutus)

...his silver hairs
Will purchase us a good opinion.
(Metellus)

Let us be sacrificers, but not butchers, Caius,
...Let's carve him as a dish fit for the gods,
Not hew him as a carcass fit for hounds.
(Brutus)

But I am as constant as the northern star.
(Caesar)

Et tu, Brute?
(Caesar)

How many ages hence
Shall this our lofty scene be acted over,
In states unborn, and accents yet unknown...
...So often shall the knot of us be called
The men that gave their country liberty.
(Cassius)

O mighty Caesar! Dost thou lie so low?
Are all thy conquests, glories, triumphs, spoils,
Shrunk to this little measure?
(Antony)

To you our swords have leaden points, Mark Antony.
(Brutus)

O pardon me, thou bleeding piece of earth,
That I am meek and gentle with these butchers...
...Cry havoc, and let slip the dogs of war.
(Antony)

...not that I loved Caesar less, but that I loved Rome more. Had you rather Caesar were living, and die all slaves, than that Caesar were dead, to live all free men? As Caesar loved me, I weep for him; as he was fortunate I rejoice at it; as he was valiant, I honour him; but, as he was ambitious, I slew him... Who is here so base, that would be a bondman? If any speak, for him have I offended.
(Brutus)

Friends, Romans, countrymen, lend me your ears;
I come to bury Caesar, not to praise him.
The evil that men do lives after them,
The good is oft interred with their bones...
...For Brutus is an honourable man,
So are they all, all honourable men...
O judgment, thou art fled to brutish beasts,
And men have lost their reason. Bear with me;
My heart is in the coffin there with Caesar,
And I must pause till it come back to me.
(Antony)

You are not wood, you are not stones, but men...
(Antony)

For Brutus, as you know, was Caesar's angel...
...This was the most unkindest cut of all.
(Antony)

Now let it work. Mischief, thou art afoot,
Take thou what course thou wilt.
(Antony)

...for we are at the stake,
And bayed about with many enemies;
And some that smile have in their hearts, I fear,
Millions of mischiefs.
(Octavius)

But hollow men, like horses hot at hand,
Make gallant show and promise of their mettle.
(Brutus)

Let me tell you, Cassius, you yourself
Are much condemned to have an itching palm.
(Brutus)

A friend should bear his friend's infirmities.
(Cassius)

There is a tide in the affairs of men,
Which, taken at the flood, leads on to fortune;
Omitted, all the voyage of their life
Is bound in shallows and in miseries.
On such a full sea are we now afloat.
(Brutus)

...thou shalt see me at Philippi.
(Caesar's ghost)

If we do meet again, why, we shall smile;
If not, why then this parting was well made...
...O, that a man might know
The end of this day's business ere it come.
(Brutus)

My heart doth joy that yet in all my life
I found no man but he was true to me.
(Brutus)

This was the noblest Roman of them all.
All the conspirators save only he
Did that they did in envy of great Caesar...
His life was gentle, and the elements
So mixed in him that Nature might stand up
And say to all the world, "This was a man."
(Antony)

MACBETH

Over the years I have had some mind-shattering theatrical experiences, and two of these are associated with *Macbeth*: the first a stormy January night in 1978 when at the Donmar Theatre I saw Ian McKellen and Judi Dench, directed by Philip Casson, and the second much more recently, when, in Chichester and in London I saw Patrick Stewart and Kate Fleetwood in the main roles, directed by Rupert Gould. It is a play which engenders tension from the very beginning with the appearance of the witches; a tension maintained throughout, even when the discovery of Duncan's murder is delayed by a comic scene with the porter talking of ushering a collection of professionals through Hell Gate, the anticipation of the horror to be revealed is thereby ratcheted up. *Macbeth* is a short play – less than half the length of *Hamlet*; yet in this concentration of narrative we have ambition, the shifting dynamics of power within a relationship, the power of the supernatural and the need for a monarch to heal and restore order, all explored through inward-looking self-exploration and through the most consistent and effective imagery of all Shakespeare's plays.

Macbeth is known by actors as 'the Scottish play', as superstition surrounds mentioning the name of the play, for Shakespeare is said to have incorporated the spells of real witches within the imprecations of the witches in the play, resulting in a curse being placed by these same real witches on productions of the play. Having said that, there is no real evidence of performances of *Macbeth* being more jinxed than any other Shakespeare play, but actors have strange rituals to ward off bad luck if *Macbeth* is mentioned, all involving the number three and maybe turning round, and maybe quoting from *The Merchant of Venice* which, conversely, is thought to be a lucky play.

Shakespeare took the story of *Macbeth* from Holinshed's *Chronicles*, published some twenty years earlier. The witches are to be found in Holinshed's story, as is the overthrow of Macbeth by Malcolm and Macduff. Banquo[74] is there too, except that in the first place he was complicit with Macbeth in the removal of Duncan. What is also different is that the 'real' Macbeth ruled for ten years and was generally thought to have been a reasonably competent and popular king. Perhaps by now it goes without saying that Shakespeare always reworks his basic material for dramatic effect.

This, then, is Shakespeare's *Macbeth*. Three witches are awaiting the arrival of Macbeth who is returning, with his fellow general Banquo, from a successful military campaign against the invading Norwegian army. The Scottish King Duncan hears of Macbeth's success and announces that Macbeth will now assume the title of the traitor Thane of Cawdor, whereupon Macbeth is greeted by the witches as Thane of Cawdor and "king hereafter". Banquo is promised that he will be the father of a line of kings. Initially Macbeth distrusts what he has heard, but he writes to his wife, telling her of the prophecy. She is preparing for a visit from King Duncan and overcomes her husband's reluctance to kill their visitor: she is not prepared to leave her husband's prospective kingship to chance. Macbeth knives to death the sleeping Duncan but it is left to Lady Macbeth to smear the sleeping grooms with Duncan's blood, thus implying their guilt. Macbeth admits, in a fury, to killing the grooms whereupon Duncan's sons, Malcolm and Donalbain, suspicious of Macbeth, flee to England and Ireland respectively, and Macbeth is crowned king at Scone. Macbeth is initially appalled at what he has done, but to secure his place on the throne he has the suspicious Banquo murdered, though Banquo's son escapes. Banquo's ghost, however, turns up at Macbeth's celebratory feast, causing consternation everywhere and, in her last moment of will-fuelled control, Lady Macbeth attempts to justify her husband's behaviour to the guests and dismisses them. From now on Macbeth pursues his killing spree without telling his wife – indeed she did not know about the planned killing of Banquo – and we witness the unprotected wife and children of Macduff butchered. Macduff had fled to England and

74   James I was descended from Banquo. Apart from dramatic considerations, it was therefore strategically good diplomacy for Shakespeare not to have Banquo involved in regicide!

we see him with Duncan's son Malcolm assembling, with the help of the English king, an army to defeat Macbeth. Prior to this Macbeth has again visited the witches and been assured that, although he should be aware of Macduff, he will never be defeated by one "of woman born", nor until "great Birnam wood to high Dunsinane hill shall come against him". Macbeth prepares to defend himself in Dunsinane; Lady Macbeth guiltily sleepwalks and then commits suicide. Malcolm gives the order for Birnam trees to be cut down and used as camouflage as they approach Dunsinane. Macbeth fears that all is lost and memorably expresses himself as disillusioned with life and his lack of friends in old age, but determines to go down fighting. He cannot avoid Macduff, who tells him that he was "from his mother's womb untimely ripp'd". Macduff kills Macbeth and the victorious Malcolm is hailed as King of Scotland, soon to be crowned at Scone.

As with the other indisputable major tragedies – *Hamlet*, *Othello*, *King Lear* – there is a central figure. As with the other major tragedies this central figure has a fatal flaw[75], which in Macbeth's case is generally accepted to be his ambition. But straightaway there must be a caveat regarding this. It is true that his startled behaviour when hailed by the witches as "king hereafter" betokens that the possibility of kingship was not a sudden new idea for Macbeth, and his wife acknowledges that he is not without ambition, but then she adds that his nature is "too full o'th'milk of human kindness" and he would be reluctant to take the easy, dishonourable route to the crown. It is worth remembering these comments from Lady Macbeth as to the fundamentally honourable nature of her husband because soon after this we, together with Macbeth, are so immersed in his bloodshed and killings that it is his insecurity and cruelty that become firmly lodged in our minds.

What changes Macbeth, of course, is his wife. She is the more ruthlessly ambitious one of the two. In the other three tragedies I

---

75   From the Greek word (used by Aristotle in his discussion of tragedy in his *Poetics*) *hamartia*. Although '*hamartia*' and 'tragic flaw' have traditionally been seen to be the same, there is some discussion today that suggests that *hamartia* actually means 'an error in judgment' or 'an ill-informed mistake'. Tragic flaw remains a valid concept, however.

mentioned in the previous paragraph each central character stands alone in so far as Ophelia, Desdemona and Cordelia are not seen as having such a close relationship, not being so privy to the private thoughts of their loved ones as is Lady Macbeth initially to her husband's. If there is a comparison to be made it is with *Antony and Cleopatra*, where their mutual exchanges are as equals. You do not get stronger women than Lady Macbeth and Cleopatra. That is a good parallel, though forcing a parallel between Banquo and Octavius, as some critics have done, is a comparison that I find a stretch too far.

Be that as it may, what we have in *Macbeth* is a fascinating dynamic between man and wife. Even when, after the banquet scene in Act 3 Scene 4, she no longer has any influence on either her husband or the action of the play Lady Macbeth cannot be forgotten, and then, memorably, she appears again in the sleepwalking scene, unable to either wash or perfume the blood from off her hands. Yes, Macbeth dominates the last two Acts but it was Lady Macbeth who powerfully instigated her husband's push for kingship and security – a role recognized fully by Malcolm at the end of the play when he speaks of "this dead butcher, and his fiend-like Queen".

It is a riveting relationship that the two of them have – the way the power switches from one to the other. Lady Macbeth sets Macbeth on his murderous course by planning the murder of Duncan; then after that Macbeth goes it alone, not even consulting his wife:

> *Be innocent of the knowledge, dearest chuck,*
> *Till thou applaud the deed.*

Their reaction to the crime of the murder of Duncan is, according to Freud[76], "like two disunited parts of a single psychical individuality". Maybe – they certainly go their separate ways emotionally speaking. What I find interesting too in their relationship is the means whereby Lady Macbeth persuades her husband to murder in the first place. She sees murder as a male activity: even before Macbeth arrives at their castle at Inverness she wishes to be unsexed – that is, to lose any womanly thoughts of tenderness and compassion – and then, when

---

76   From Freud's *Some Character Types met with in Psychoanalytical Work* (1916).

Macbeth utters his last doubts about the killing she taunts him with being less than a man if he will not kill. And once he succumbs to Lady Macbeth's taunting and daring, Macbeth too passes comment on what it is to be male, when he expresses the belief that a woman of such "undaunted mettle" as his wife should only give birth to "men-children". When at the end of Act 4 Macduff hears of the slaughter of his wife and children he knows that he "could play the woman with my eyes" but in reality wants to confront Macbeth with his sword as soon as possible. Malcolm sees this as a "manly" response. This acceptance of fighting and killing as male attributes is implicit in *Macbeth*. Plus ça change?

There is a consistency in the exploring of masculinity in *Macbeth*. What is also remarkable is – more than in any other of Shakespeare's plays – the consistency of the imagery; the most notable image being the clothes one: the idea that Macbeth is always wearing someone else's clothes and they do not fit him. For example, the "borrow'd robes" of Cawdor as seen by Banquo as "strange garments" that do not fit Macbeth, and in Act 5 in the words of Angus: "…now does he feel his title / Hang loose about him, like a giant's robe / Upon a dwarfish thief". In between these two references there are many more examples of ill-fitting clothing imagery.

Similarly there are so many blood references in *Macbeth*. Memorably, Macbeth talks of wading through a sea of blood; Duncan, according to Lady Macbeth has "so much blood in him"; Macbeth sees his first act of bloodshed as dyeing a whole ocean red; Banquo's ghost has "gory locks"; neither Lady Macbeth not Macbeth can ever remove the blood from their hands. And so on – the play is steeped in blood. There is a good deal of light-and-dark imagery too, and all in all there is a mood of blood and fear and darkness and terror, maintained by the wonderful imagery.

What I think is also remarkable about *Macbeth* is the quality of the soliloquys. Of course Lear has some great insights into the nature of society and Hamlet rarely short-changes himself when it comes to introspection. Almost certainly the most referenced soliloquy of all is Hamlet's "To be or not to be" speech, but for its sustainment of a resigned mood and the depth of its commentary on life I prefer Macbeth's "Tomorrow and tomorrow and tomorrow" speech. In fact I like it so much that I have included it in its entirety in the Memorable Quotations section at the end of this essay – every single word is weighted and counts. And this is by far not the only memorable soliloquy in *Macbeth*: "Two truths are told"; "If it were done"; "Is this a dagger, which I see before me?"; "Thou hast it now"; "To be thus is nothing"; "Come, seeling Night"; "Time, thou anticipat'st my dread exploits"; "I have liv'd long enough" – all these lines presage a heart-searching soliloquy. In addition we have Lady Macbeth's "The raven himself is hoarse, / That croaks the fatal entrance of Duncan / Under my battlements."

And what soliloquys do above all else is to help us understand the workings of the protagonist's mind and thereby create or extend our sympathy for him/her. On the surface Macbeth is a regicide who, in order to secure his power and domination, goes on a callous killing spree to the detriment of the wellbeing of his country. His mind might be poisoned – by the witches and his wife – but there still is no excuse for his actions and no requirement of sympathy for him. Yet we are privy to his innermost doubts and fears; we know the soul-searching and ultimately the disappointment experienced by Macbeth. We might not like the man but we have journeyed with him and, in essence, he has shared intimacies with us. All done by soliloquy. In Shakespeare's hands Macbeth is not merely a black-hearted killer driven on by nothing but ruthless ambition – he is also a human whom we can recognise.

Macbeth is always remembered for the witches, the unnatural hags who appear to be neither female nor male, neither human nor supernatural. They embody ambiguity: you are not sure what you see. As such they immediately set the tone of untrustworthiness within the play: "Fair is foul, and foul is fair" they chant, long before Duncan speaks, ironically to Macbeth, of his misplaced trust in the Thane of Cawdor – "There's no art / To find the mind's construction in the face." A modern audience does not believe in the evil of witchcraft, but a Shakespearean audience did. Queen Elizabeth's Witchcraft Act of 1562 outlawed "all manner of Conjuracions, Inchantmentes and Witchcraftes" and, at the likely time Shakespeare was writing *Macbeth*, James I added to it in 1604. There were two hundred and seventy witchcraft trials in Elizabethan England, two hundred and forty-seven of them being of women, almost exclusively being the elderly, single or widowed[77]. Scapegoats were needed for unaccountable disasters such as plagues, and 'witches' were vulnerable. The point is, though, that Shakespeare's audience would not in the least have been discommoded by the presentation of witches on stage, and they certainly contribute hugely to Macbeth's temptation and his downfall, and, from curtain-rise, the mood of darkness and evil in *Macbeth* is set. And there have been suggestions that when Lady Macbeth calls on the "spirits that tend on mortal thoughts" to unsex her she is in fact revealing herself as a black witch.

There is some white magic in *Macbeth* too; I refer to the scene in England at the end of Act 4. Fundamentally this scene is Malcolm testing Macduff to see if he truly is opposed to Macbeth. Personally I find this scene overlong as it stalls the momentum towards resolution, and one of the reasons for its slowness is the interpolation of a speech (based on Holinshed's account of Edward the Confessor's healing powers) about the good English king and how he possesses both a "healing benediction" and "a heavenly gift of prophesy". This is meant, and undoubtedly seen, as praise for James I who believed that *he* possessed such gifts. Shakespeare, of the King's Players, knows on which side his bread is buttered, and is thereby not averse to flattery.

Before I conclude, there are two other features of *Macbeth* that we find in other Shakespeare plays, maintaining his world view. In *Julius Caesar* Casca reports "a civil strife in heaven" and tame lions walking the streets, and owls hooting and shrieking at noon-day – all unnatural occurrences and all presaging something unnatural to follow in the social order. And after the murder of Duncan in *Macbeth*, a seventy-year-old man and Ross talk of darkness covering the earth during the day, of a mousing owl killing a falcon and Duncan's horses breaking loose and eating each other. A great perturbation in nature. Unnatural acts – the killing of a ruler – disrupt the natural world too; this natural world echoes and parallels the political world and when

---

77   Elizabethan statute did forbid the use of torture to obtain confession – unlike George W. Bush's condoning such practices – and it is noteworthy that in the 17th century the Catholic church equated all herbal gathering with witchcraft. The last Papal Ordinance against witchcraft came from Gregory XV in 1623.

there is something rotten in the state, be it of Denmark or elsewhere, nature is also unnatural and turbulent. It could be argued too that Macbeth's (and demonstratively his wife's) lacking "the season of all nature's Sleep… great Nature's second course" is another example of how unnatural deeds beget unnatural consequences.

Finally Shakespeare restores, as he always does, order at the end of *Macbeth*: Macbeth is dead, Malcolm is hailed as King of Scotland, exiled friends are called back from abroad and Malcolm goes to Scone to be crowned in the tradition of Scottish kings. In many ways that is all there is to say, but I want to mention a brilliant *coup de théâtre* in Roman Polanski's 1971 film of *Macbeth*. The film is usually remembered for its excesses of bloodshed, and for Francesca Annis playing Lady Macbeth's sleepwalking scene naked. For me, though, it was what Polanski did with Donalbain. In the play Donalbain does little except to agree with his elder brother Malcolm that to stay in Scotland is unsafe; so he flies to Ireland and that's all we hear of him. Polanski early in his film establishes him as a dwarfish, hunchbacked figure, and then in the very last shots we see the silhouette of his figure trudging up the hills to where Macbeth had his encounters with the witches. Brilliant!

That's it. With the possible exception of *King Lear*, *Macbeth* hits you more viscerally than any other Shakespeare play. From curtain-up it is full of darkness, menace and distrust. We experience Macbeth's heart of darkness and the horror at the centre of it. "Light thickens" and as "good things of day begin to droop and drowse" deeds of "dreadful note" are done. We are privy to it all, including the torture in Macbeth's mind. The imagery, the action and the characterisation are all knitted skilfully together. Seeing *Macbeth* is a great experience.

Memorable Quotations From *Macbeth*

When shall we three meet again?
In thunder, lightning or in rain?
(Witches)

Fair is foul and foul is fair.
(Witches)

Were such things here, as we do speak about,
Or have we eaten on the insane root?
(Banquo)

And oftentimes to win us to our harm,
The instruments of Darkness tell us truths;
Win us with honest trifles, to betray's
In deepest consequence.
(Banquo)

Come what come may
Time and the hour runs through the roughest day.
(Macbeth)

To beguile the time,
Look like the time…
Look like th'innocent flower,
But be the serpent under't.
(Lady Macbeth)

Woulds't thou have that
Which thou esteem'st the ornament of life,
And live a coward in thine own esteem,
Letting "I dare not" wait upon "I would",
Like the poor cat i'th'adage?
(Lady Macbeth)

But screw your courage to the sticking-place,
And we'll not fail.
(Lady Macbeth)

False face must hide what the false heart doth know.
(Macbeth)

I go, and it is done: the bell invites me.
Hear it not, Duncan; for it is a knell
That summons thee to Heaven or to Hell.
(Macbeth)

Will all great Neptune's ocean wash this blood
Clean from my hand? No, this my hand will rather
The multitudinous seas incarnadine,
Making the green one red.
(Macbeth)

A little water clears us of this deed.
(Lady Macbeth)

What... does drink especially provoke?
(Macduff)
Lechery, Sir, it provokes, and unprovokes: it provokes desire, but it takes
away the performance.
(Porter)

There's daggers in men's smiles.
(Donalbain)

Ay, in the catalogue ye go for men.
(Macbeth)

O! full of scorpions is my mind, dear wife!
(Macbeth)

Good things of Day begin to droop and drowse…
Things bad begun make strong themselves by ill.
(Macbeth)

But now, I am cabin'd, cribb'd, confin'd, bound in
To saucy doubts and fears.
(Macbeth)

Stand not upon the order of your going,
But go at once.
(Lady Macbeth)

I am in blood
Stepp'd in so far, that, should I wade no more,
Returning were as tedious as go o'er…
We are yet but young in deed.
(Macbeth)

Double, double, toil and trouble:
Fire, burn; and, cauldron, bubble.
(Witches)

From this moment,
The very firstlings of my heart shall be
The firstlings of my hand.
(Macbeth)

But, I have none: the king-becoming graces,
As Justice, Verity, Temp'rance, Stableness,
Bounty, Perseverance, Mercy, Lowliness,
Devotion, Patience, Courage, Fortitude,
I have no relish of them…
(Malcolm)

But I have words,
That would be howl'd out in the desert air,
Where hearing should not latch them.
(Ross)

The night is long that never finds the day.
(Malcolm)

Out, damn'd spot!... Hell is murky... Yet who would have thought the
old man to have had so much blood in him? What, will these hands ne'er
be clean?... all the perfumes of Arabia will not sweeten this little hand...
What's done cannot be undone.
(Lady Macbeth)

The devil damn thee black, thou cream-fac'd loon!
(Macbeth)

...my way of life
Is fall'n into the sere, the yellow leaf;
And that which should accompany old age,
As honour, love, obedience, troops of friends,
I must not look to have.
(Macbeth)

To-morrow, and to-morrow, and to-morrow,
Creeps in this petty pace from day to day,
To the last syllable of recorded time:
And all our yesterdays have lighted fools
The way to dusty death. Out, out, brief candle!
Life's but a walking shadow; a poor player,
That struts and frets his hour upon the stage,
And then is heard no more: it is a tale,
Told by an idiot, full of sound and fury,
Signifying nothing.
(Macbeth)

They have tied me to a stake: I cannot fly,
But bear-like, I must fight the course.
(Macbeth)

...lay on, Macduff;
And damn'd be him that first cries, "Hold enough!"
(Macbeth)

HAMLET

Everyone knows *Hamlet*. Everyone has her/his interpretation, probably running along similar lines but with personal nuances. Freud too wrote memorably about Hamlet as an example of his Oedipal complex theory. Throughout the world it is the most performed of Shakespeare's plays. It is easily the longest of Shakespeare's plays and has the most quoted lines – indeed if anyone asks you what Shakespeare play a particular quotation comes from and you do not know, say *Hamlet* and the chances are that you will be right. It really is a wonderful play, with actors straining at the leash to play the main role – most recently Jude Law and David Tennant, more famous for their screen acting, have joined the list of Hamlet performers and brought their fans with them, thus introducing Shakespeare to a new audience. Is there anyone in the English-speaking world – and maybe beyond – who has not heard of *Hamlet*? That is a claim that, I think, could not be made about any other Shakespeare play.

What makes this a great play? First of all it is a damn good story – with a 'will he/won't he' dilemma at the centre of it. It's about sex, murder and revenge. There is a ghost; spies everywhere creating an atmosphere of distrust; there are philosophical issues about the nature of life, suicide, the nature of man and fate raised. And at the centre of it is this perplexed young man, emotionally torn every which way and yet at the same time having an enormous obligation and responsibility placed on him. My first *Hamlet* was the Peter Hall 1965 RSC production, about which Hall wrote: "For our decade, I think the play will be about the disillusionment which produces an apathy of the will so deep that that commitment to politics, to religion or to life is impossible." David Warner's Hamlet, with his long, rust-red scarf, captured this student disillusionment almost perfectly. Since then I have seen Ben Kingsley, Jonathan Pryce, Alan Bates, Simon Russell Beale, Ben Wishaw and Rory Kinnear, amongst others, play Hamlet and all have brought something fresh and relevant to the role.

The basic story of *Hamlet* had been around for centuries. It's a Danish story that had previously been orally retold – and therefore embellished – but which was finally nailed in writing by Saxo Grammaticus in his *Historia Danica* late in the 12th century and then printed in Paris in 1514. The differences between the Grammaticus story and Shakespeare's are not great: Grammaticus does not have a ghost and in his version the equivalent of Polonius is dismembered and thrown into an open latrine, where wild hogs devour his corpse! The possibility of the Queen's having committed adultery is also not in Grammaticus.

This, then, is the story of Shakespeare's *Hamlet*. Soldiers on watch at the castle of Elsinore see what they believe to be the recently deceased King's ghost. This would seem to indicate that "Something is rotten in the state of Denmark." Horatio, Hamlet's friend, persuades Hamlet to come the next night to the battlements, where he confronts the ghost. It *is* the ghost of his father, who tells Hamlet something of which Hamlet had already had forebodings – that he was murdered while he slept in his orchard and that the murderer was his brother, who then married Hamlet's mother and was crowned king. Hamlet is exhorted to avenge his father's murder. Hamlet thus knows what he has to do, but has philosophical and psychological problems with killing his uncle and contemplates suicide as a way out. We know that Hamlet has been a soldier, scholar and courtier of great eminence from his girlfriend Ophelia's description of him, but now, perhaps to buy time, he feigns madness. Hamlet's uncle, the new King Claudius, sets on Polonius (Ophelia's father and Lord Chamberlain) and Hamlet's old 'friends' Rosencrantz and Guildenstern to spy on Hamlet for "madness in great ones must not unwatched go". (Polonius also sends someone to spy on his son Laertes as to how he is behaving at university!) Under instructions from her father, Ophelia attempts to return Hamlet's gifts, causing Hamlet further disillusionment with women; Polonius believes that Hamlet's mad behaviour is brought about by his love for Ophelia but Claudius is not satisfied with this reason. Hamlet enlists a troupe of travelling players to enact a play very like his father's murder, and Claudius rises in anger before the end of the play, thereby cementing in Hamlet's mind that his father's ghost was an honest ghost. Still, though, he does not kill Claudius, even though a young Norwegian prince, Fortinbras, sets him an example of valour and even though he comes upon his uncle praying – a kneeling target. Hamlet confronts his mother in her closet where Polonius is spying behind an arras: Polonius utters a sound and instinctively Hamlet stabs him through the arras and kills him, and then is disappointed that the dead man was not the King.

Ophelia loses her sanity and drowns herself, and Hamlet allows himself to be shipped off to England with Rosencrantz and Guildenstern, the latter two carrying letters ordering the King of England to kill Hamlet. By chance (?)[78], pirates set upon Hamlet's ship and in the fight, Hamlet boards the pirates' boat and they land him back in Denmark. Here he encounters Ophelia's funeral. Laertes, with his father and sister being recently deceased, has returned from his university studies in Paris, demanding explanations from the King. Hamlet and Laertes have to be pulled apart over Ophelia's grave and the King blames all Laertes' family woes on Hamlet. The King arranges a fencing match between Hamlet and Laertes in which Laertes is fighting with a poison-envenomed sword and the backup of a poisoned chalice which can be offered to Hamlet. In the course of the fight swords are exchanged so that both Hamlet and Laertes are fatally wounded, and the Queen drinks from the poisoned cup. Laertes understands what has happened, forgives Hamlet, and Hamlet at last kills Claudius. Horatio is entrusted with telling Hamlet's story and Fortinbras arrives to eulogise Hamlet and become King of Denmark.

That is the story, and of course everything in the play centres around the character of Hamlet. Yes, he procrastinates but the big question is why he does so. Very relevant is the attraction of suicide which he evinces immediately in his first soliloquy in Act 1 Scene 2: "O that this too solid flesh would melt " he wishes, and then regrets that "the Everlasting had not fixed his canon 'gainst self-slaughter".

---

78   There is some speculation that when Hamlet refers to "when in one line two crafts directly meet" in his speech at the very end of the third Act, this indicates that he had planned the pirate ship's interception of the ship taking him to England. Considering Hamlet's state of mind, I think this is unlikely.

Later the whole "To be or not to be" soliloquy makes a clear case for the suffering mind to relieve itself of the buffets and heartaches of fortune through suicide were it not for the fear of what awaits us when we die – "the undiscovered country".

In the "To be or not to be" speech Hamlet makes no mention of the morality of a revenge killing of his uncle, the new king; obviously that is part of the burden of living which he wishes to shed but *Hamlet* is far more than a play focused solely on the issue of revenge. In this most famous of soliloquys Hamlet puts his inaction down to "conscience" making him cowardly. It is important at this juncture to realize that in this context 'conscience' has the meaning of introspection, of thinking too much. We have the – trusted, I think – word of Ophelia that before the play began Hamlet was, par excellence, a fashionable and charming courtier, a soldier and a scholar, yet, with the exception of his showing a few fencing skills in his duel with Laertes, none of these attributes are remotely apparent in the play – indeed quite the converse. As Ophelia says: "O, woe is me / 'T'have seen what I have seen, see what I see!" So what has caused this descent into madness; this stultifying introversion which prevents Hamlet from killing Claudius, even when the ready opportunity arises as Claudius, undefended, prays? It is a feigned madness Hamlet adopts – a madness behind which he hides in order to buy time – but he chooses the mask or cover which comes most easily to him. What he has experienced completely shatters any equilibrium he might have had. His father has died and his mother, within a very short span of time – two months – has married Hamlet's father's brother. Even before he meets his father's ghost he is finding the situation nigh on emotionally impossible. Then he is exhorted to avenge his father's murder. On top of all this he is aware of his every move being watched, and his girlfriend returns his gifts to him. It is no wonder that in all these circumstances Hamlet's emotional exhaustion leads to inaction.

It is very much thinking too much about things that prevents Hamlet acting. When Polonius cries for help from behind the arras in Gertrude's chamber, Hamlet instinctively thrusts through the arras and kills him – there was no time for thought. But thinking is very much a natural part of Hamlet's being: he is thirty years of age and, until brought home by the death of his father, he was studying at the University of Wittenberg. We do not know what Hamlet was studying[79] but years spent at university inevitably develop logical reasoning and place a premium on the power of thought. Yet Hamlet was a comparatively young man: he still has "the heyday in [his] blood". We can sense his sexual abhorrence of his mother's liaison with his uncle when he speaks of "the rank sweat of an enseamed bed" and "the bloat king" pinching "wanton on your cheek" and "paddling in your neck with his damned fingers". Undoubtedly too it is a sexual relationship (and a loving one) that Hamlet enjoyed with Ophelia: they both know what "country matters" mean and Ophelia's mad song is full of both sexual innuendo and explicit sexual comments. Women turning away from him for no acceptable reason – clearly he has no truck with Polonius' assertion to his daughter that "Lord Hamlet is a prince out of thy star" – further exacerbates Hamlet's profound distress. Ophelia becomes tarred with the same brush as his mother: "Frailty thy name is woman." The only fit place for women is a "nunnery" which, as well as its established meaning, was also contemporary slang for a brothel.

Before we consider the factors that caused Hamlet's development from a man railing against his perceived fate to a man accepting his fate, a word or two about Freud. Freud[80] wrote extensively about Hamlet. For him he was a splendid example of his Oedipus complex theory – just as dreams disguise unconscious realities, he argued, so Hamlet used his madness to disguise the truth that he had a repressed sexual desire for his mother (witness the explosive intimacy of the scene together in her chamber). Claudius was thus acting out Hamlet's own fantasies – which disgusted him – and therefore killing Claudius was tantamount to killing himself. If this is even partly the reason for his sloth in the killing of Claudius it certainly ties in with Hamlet's brooding on and contemplating suicide. An interesting theory.

So, finally, in this consideration of the character of Hamlet, what does enable him to act against the King? His "special providence[81]

79   When Hamlet says: "There are more things in heaven and earth, Horatio, / Than are dreamt of in your philosophy" it does not, of course, indicate that either of them studied Philosophy.
80   In *The Interpretation of Dreams* (on *Hamlet*), 1900.
81   Calvin, in his writing about predestination, frequently used the

in the fall of a sparrow speech", when he accepts the combat with Laertes, is the sign of a Hamlet who no longer wishes to avoid what is now seen as an inevitable destiny. The process by which he has come to this realisation is, I think, begun when he hears the Player King's Hecuba speech; it continues with his killing Polonius in his mother's closet; then we have Fortinbras observed marching against the Polack "to gain a little patch of ground / That hath in it no profit but the name". It is a slow journey of self-realisation, though, for although he says after seeing Fortinbras' army that "from this time forth / My thoughts be bloody, or be nothing worth", Hamlet allows himself to be shipped to England. The pirate ship is a providential intervention for Hamlet, and this, followed by his being reminded of the "fellow of infinite jest" Yorick, who has been in his grave for decades, and his witnessing the burial of Ophelia – "Now get you to my lady's chamber, and tell her, let her paint an inch thick, to this favour she must come" – all leads Hamlet to a realisation of the inescapability of his fate. It is a sane, mature acceptance of life as it is: he accepts the fencing challenge, makes peace with Laertes and only turns on the King when the dying Laertes reveals the plot against his life. Hamlet dies and "the rest is silence", but we have been on a rollercoaster of a journey with one of the most fascinating characters in literature. There are other facets of the play which I will briefly comment on. It is Hamlet the Dane, though, who fundamentally matters.

---

analogy of the stage, where all parts were written for the performers, thereby implying we all have a predestined script to follow. Shakespeare's Hamlet was studying at Wittenberg, where Martin Luther taught from 1508 until his death in 1546. (The university was in fact founded only in 1508, so Shakespeare, ignoring authenticity, has chosen Wittenberg deliberately.) And there may be an in-joke when Hamlet, after the killing of Polonius, refers to "a certain convocation of politic worms"- Worms being the place where Luther was declared a heretic in 1521. Predestination, though, was a sensitive subject and although in "the special providence in the fall of a sparrow" speech, there is clearly a reference to an acceptance of what may well be a preordained fate, it should be noted that the reference has been watered down in the Folio edition: in the Quarto we read "there's a predestinate providence in the fall of a sparrow". Censorship?

There is a good deal of consistent imagery in *Hamlet*. In her *Shakespeare's Imagery, and what it tells us* (1935) Caroline Spurgeon sees an ulcerous cancer as the dominant theme; it stems from the real poisoning of Hamlet's father while he slept, and from Marcellus' confident announcement that "Something is rotten in the state of Denmark" onwards we have examples of "a mole in nature". There is the "unweeded garden", the "canker [that] galls the infants of the spring", "the foul and pestilent congregation of vapours". Hamlet exhorts his mother to "not spread the compost on the weeds / To make them ranker". All images of a nature that it is out of control, a spreading cancerous sickness everywhere. Most effective too is Hamlet's accusation that Rosencrantz and Guildenstern wish to play upon him as if he were a pipe. In addition there are the images of sexual revulsion that I have mentioned in connection with Gertrude and Ophelia, reinforced by Hamlet's whipping himself with the accusatory words of being a whore and a drab and a scullion[82] in his speech at the end of Act Scene 2. Denmark and its inhabitants and their values are consistently presented as diseased, with nature being perverted.

You cannot trust anyone in the Denmark of Claudius, Gertrude and Polonius. Claudius and Polonius spy on the meeting between Hamlet and Ophelia; Guildenstern and Rosencrantz are commissioned to spy on Hamlet and report back to Claudius and Gertrude; Polonius meets his death when secreted behind an arras listening to the dialogue between Hamlet and his mother. And, of course, Polonius even sends Reynaldo to spy on his son Laertes, to find out what he is up to while studying in Paris. One of the most effective productions of *Hamlet* that I have seen was that of the Nottingham Playhouse in 1971, directed by Anthony Page, with Alan Bates in the lead role, as the stage was covered in mirrors, indicating how all movements were reflected and noticed elsewhere. It wasn't just all occasions that informed against Hamlet.

Hamlet exemplifies many Shakespearean ploys which by now are recognizable – the time sequence for example. As ever in the theatre we experience a consecutive series of events as though they

---

82   "Scullion" – a kitchen wench – is from the Folio edition. The Quarto used "stallion" – a male prostitute. Either way there is a sexual distaste.

happen, pat, one after another in rapid succession. But in the real world, as distinct from the world of the theatre, this is rarely so. One outstanding example of this is the sending to and the return from Norway of the Danish ambassadors. In reality we are talking weeks and probably months, which extends the period of Hamlet's dilatory doubting considerably more than the theatre audience experiences.

Before we consider the essential meaning of *Hamlet* there are a couple of things that interest me. One is the revenge theme and how it compares with *The Tempest*. As we have seen, Prospero makes the decision to forgive his enemies at the end of the play, whereas in *Hamlet*, written some dozen years earlier, there is no question of there being any forgiveness. Had the plays been written in reverse order, would there have been different endings? The crimes perpetrated against Prospero and Hamlet do differ considerably but I just wonder if, with the same basic story of *Hamlet*, Shakespeare may have changed the outcome…

The outcome, or the ending, sees Fortinbras returning to Denmark and claiming the crown thereof. Shakespeare always wants order to be restored at the end of his plays and so we have it, with Fortinbras having Hamlet's dying support. But there is the delicious irony of this military man, who acts without a scruple of thought, pronouncing on "the prince of philosophical speculation" (Hazlitt), and, in death, giving him military honours.

So, what do we take away with us from our reading or watching *Hamlet*? There are moral values expressed in Polonius' "these few precepts in thy memory" speech. They come across glibly as simple platitudes but I would not discount that there is some value in them, even though Polonius is far from an attractive character and is usually portrayed as a meddling buffoon. But it is what Hamlet says and does that matters – therein lie the values we take from the play. T. S. Eliot called *Hamlet* "an artistic failure", which runs counter to the experience of almost everyone who has seen a good production of the play. We have been witness to a young man's moral dilemma and struggle; we have experienced with him the disintegration of his world around him and of his inner world. There have been no easy answers, such as those Polonius trotted out in the aforementioned speech. Life is a struggle. The world can be a foul and corrupt place, at times apparently possessed entirely by "things gross and rank in nature". But there is another way of looking at the world and mankind, a way Hamlet perceives and expresses: "What a piece of work is man, how noble in reason, how infinite in faculties, in form and moving how express and admirable, in action how like an angel, in apprehension how like a god: the beauty of the world, the paragon of animals..." The world does not have to be "a sterile promontory", man does not have to be "this quintessence of dust". Through sharing with Hamlet all the doubts about the morality of revenge, the shattering of his life, the heart-searching and then the final acceptance of his fate and obligation, we have shared this admirable young man's journey. The things that are humanly important win through at the end: I refer to his undoubted love for Ophelia, his love for his mother, his upholding of the pledge he made to his father's ghost, his trusted friendship with Horatio and his reconciliation with Laertes. "What a piece of work" is Hamlet and *Hamlet*!

Memorable Quotations From *Hamlet*

For this relief much thanks.
(Francisco)

And then it started, like a guilty thing
Upon a fearful summons.
(Horatio)

A little more than kin and less than kind.
(Hamlet)

O that this too too sullied flesh would melt,
Thaw, and resolve itself into a dew…
How weary, stale, flat, and unprofitable
Seem to me all the uses of this world…
…frailty, thy name is woman.
(Hamlet)

'A was a man, take him for all in all,
I shall not look upon his like again.
(Hamlet)

A countenance more in sorrow than in anger.
(Horatio)

And these few precepts in thy memory…
Give every man thine ear, but few thy voice…
Neither a borrower nor a lender be…
This above all, to thine own self be true,
And it must follow, as the night the day,
Thou canst not then be false to any man.
(Polonius)

...it is a custom
More honoured in the breach than the observance.
(Hamlet)

Something is rotten in the state of Denmark.
(Marcellus)

That one may smile, and smile, and be a villain!
(Hamlet)

There are more things in heaven and earth, Horatio,
Than are dreamt of in your philosophy.
(Hamlet)

The time is out of joint. O cursed spite
That ever I was born to set it right!
(Hamlet)

More matter, with less art.
(Queen)

Ay, sir. To be honest, as this world goes, is to be one man picked out of ten
thousand.
(Hamlet)

Though this be madness, yet there is method in't.
(Polonius)

...there is nothing either good or bad but thinking makes it so.
(Hamlet)

O God, I could be bounded in a nutshell and count myself a king of infinite
space, were it not that I have bad dreams.
(Hamlet)

I have of late, but wherefore I know not, lost all my mirth... This goodly frame, the earth, seems to me a sterile promontory... What a piece of work is a man, how noble in reason, how infinite in faculties... The beauty of the world, the paragon of animals; and yet to me, what is this quintessence of dust?
(Hamlet)

I am but mad north-northwest: when the wind is southerly I know a hawk from a handsaw.
(Hamlet)

...for this play... pleased not the million; 'twas caviare to the general.
(Hamlet)

Use every man after his desert, and who shall scape whipping?
(Hamlet)

O, what a rogue and peasant slave am I!...
...What's Hecuba to him, or he to Hecuba,
That he should weep for her?...
But I am pigeon-livered and lack gall...
...The play's the thing
Wherein I'll catch the conscience of the King.
(Hamlet)

To be, or not to be: that is the question:...
...To die, to sleep –
To sleep – perchance to dream: ay, there's the rub...
For who would bear the whips and scorns of time...
When he himself might his quietus make
With a bare bodkin?...
But that the dread of something after death,
The undiscovered country, from whose bourn
No traveller returns, puzzles the will...
Thus conscience does make cowards of us all.
(Hamlet)

Get thee to a nunnery. Why wouldst thou be a breeder of sinners?
(Hamlet)

O what a noble mind is here o'erthrown!
...O woe is me
T' have seen what I have seen, see what I see!
(Ophelia)

There's something in his soul
O'er which his melancholy sits on brood.
(King)

Madness in great ones must not unwatched go.
(King)

...let your own discretion be your tutor. Suit the action to the word, the word to the action... the purpose of playing... was and is... to hold, as 'twere, the mirror up to nature.
(Hamlet)

The lady doth protest too much, methinks.
(Queen)

...They do but jest, poison in jest.
(Hamlet)

Let me be cruel, but not unnatural;
I will speak daggers to her, but use none.
(Hamlet)

You cannot call it love, for at your age
The heyday in the blood is tame, it's humble,
And waits upon the judgment.
(Hamlet)

For 'tis the sport to have the engineer
Hoist with his own petard.
(Hamlet)

How all occasions do inform against me
…Rightly to be great
Is not to stir without great argument,
But greatly to find quarrel in a straw
When honour's at the stake…
…O, from this time forth,
My thoughts be bloody, or be nothing worth!
(Hamlet)

Good night, ladies, good night. Sweet ladies, good night, good night.
(Ophelia)

When sorrows come, they come not in single spies,
But in battalions.
(King)

There's rosemary, that's for remembrance. Pray you, love, remember. And
there is pansies, that's for thoughts.
(Ophelia)

And where th'offence is, let the great axe fall.
(King)

They have dealt with me like thieves of mercy.
(Horatio, reading Hamlet's letter)

Or are you like the painting of a sorrow,
A face without a heart?
(King)

Too much of water hast thou, poor Ophelia.
(Laertes)

Alas, poor Yorick! I knew him, Horatio, a fellow of infinite jest… Now get
you to my lady's chamber, and tell her, let her paint an inch thick, to this
favour, she must come.
(Hamlet)

I loved Ophelia. Forty thousand brothers
Could not with all their quantity of love
Make up my sum.
(Hamlet)

Let Hercules himself do what he may,
The cat will mew, and dog will have his day.
(Hamlet)

There's a divinity that shapes our ends,
Rough-hew them how we will.
(Hamlet)

Not a whit, we defy augury. There is special providence in the fall of a
sparrow. If it be not now, 'tis not to come; if it be not to come, it will be now;
if it be not now, yet it will come. The readiness is all.
(Hamlet)

A hit, a very palpable hit!
(Osric)

But I do propesy th'election lights
On Fortinbras. He has my dying voice…
…the rest is silence.
(Hamlet)

Now cracks a noble heart. Good night, sweet Prince,
And flights of angels sing thee to thy rest.
(Horatio)

Let four captains
Bear Hamlet like a soldier to the stage,
For he was likely, had he put on,
To have proved most royal.
(Fortinbras)